Jewish Settlers
— in the —
Arizona
Territory

Jewish Settlers
— in the —
Arizona
Territory

Blaine Lamb

THE
History
PRESS

Published by The History Press
Charleston, SC
www.historypress.com

First published 2023

Manufactured in the United States

ISBN 9781467154659

Library of Congress Control Number: 2023940717

CONTENTS

It was a sunny Friday morning in 1873, and William Zeckendorf stood in the doorway of his Tucson store. He adjusted his spectacles and brushed away the adobe dust that seemed to find its way into every nook and cranny in the Old Pueblo. Today, however, William had other things on his mind besides selling merchandise. He set aside his shopkeeper's apron and dressed in black. He was on his way to a funeral and then to a lynching—a lynching he would lead. In the remote Gila River valley a few years later, Anna Solomon tended the family's general store and hotel while her husband, Isadore, cut timber and burned and hauled charcoal to supply furnaces at the rich Clifton copper mines owned by her cousin Henry Lesinsky. In the growing agricultural community of Phoenix in 1874, young Morris Goldwater sat in the telegraph office in his father's store, sending and receiving the dots and dashes that kept the town in touch with the outside world. About the same time, Ike Levy navigated his barge, the Black Crook, *around the treacherous shoals and sand bars of the Colorado River. These were true pioneers, and they were Jews whose journeys took them away from the farms, villages and cities of Europe and the East Coast, to the American wilderness where they settled a new territory—Arizona.*

ACKNOWLEDGEMENTS

A number of individuals and institutions contributed to the completion of this book. The work is derived from my doctoral dissertation in history that I completed at Arizona State University over forty years ago. Because of this time gap, almost all of the persons listed below who helped me with the structuring and research have passed on. Nonetheless, I wish to thank my graduate committee and its chair, Dr. Robert Trennert. I also owe a debt of gratitude to Mr. Bert Fireman and Mrs. Susie Sato of the Arizona Historical Foundation, then located in the Hayden Library at ASU, and to a friend and colleague, Dr. Geoffrey Mawn.

The staffs of several libraries and archives proved most helpful in my original research, bringing that research up to date, and locating graphic materials. I particularly wish to thank the staffs of the Arizona Historical Society and University of Arizona Special Collections in Tucson; the Arizona Collection at ASU; Arizona Department of Library; Archives and Public Records in Phoenix; the Sharlot Hall Museum Library and Archives in Prescott, Arizona; the Museum of Northern Arizona in Flagstaff, Arizona; and the Navajo County Historical Society in Holbrook, Arizona. I am grateful to the staffs of the San Diego Historical Society Library, California State Library in Sacramento, the Bancroft Library at the University of California–Berkeley and the American Jewish Archives in Cincinnati, Ohio.

I also wish to acknowledge the support of the late Rabbi Albert Plotkin, and his late wife, Sylvia, of Congregation Beth Israel in Phoenix, who developed the idea of writing a history of the Jews of early Arizona and convinced this graduate student to undertake it.

I would be remiss if I did not extend a sincere thanks to Dr. Lawrence Bell, executive director of the Arizona Jewish Historical Society at the Cutler-Plotkin Jewish Heritage Center in Phoenix for his support of this project. Thanks also to Martin Richelsoph, the society's archivist, who made available and copied a wealth of historic photographs, many of which appear in this book. Two other individuals deserve mention as well: Dr. Joseph Tuscano, oncologist at the University of California–Davis Medical Center, who has kept me around long enough to write my books, and inquires about the progress on this book every time I see him. Dr. John Langellier, retired U.S. government historian (and former college roommate), let me tag along on some of his research trips so I could do a bit of my own research.

The biggest thanks, however, go to my wife, Rosemary, who has constantly encouraged me to complete this project, accompanied me on my research trips and has been generous in sharing the computer.

1

THE PIONEERS

Nathan Benjamin Appel

Nathan Benjamin Appel first saw Tucson in 1856, and for the next three decades, the fortunes of Arizona's first identified settler would be tied to the development of the territory. An unlikely character to have been Arizona's pioneer Jew—he did not practice Judaism or any other religion, for that matter. But when Appel died, a rabbi may have prayed over his grave.

Nathan Appel was born in Hochstadt am Main in Germany on April 14, 1828. He immigrated to the United States while still a teenager. After a brief stay in New York, in 1846 Nathan moved on to St. Louis, Missouri. The streets bustled with soldiers and wagon freighters preparing for the invasion of northern Mexico and the conquest of California. He initially tried to enlist in one of the volunteer mounted units then forming as part of Stephen Watts Kearney's Army of the West but could not find a suitable horse. Rather than trudging across the plains as an infantryman, he joined an army contract freighter as a teamster and soon was off down the Santa Fe Trail.

Nathan arrived safely in Santa Fe in 1847, a year after its bloodless conquest by Kearney. The town seemed exotic and a place he wanted to stay, at least for a while. With money from the teamstering job, he purchased a wagon and team along with some clothing and household goods. He then embarked on a number of trading ventures to the villages around Santa Fe, selling his merchandise to the Indian Pueblos, Hispanic herders and Anglo ranchers at what he admitted was a "very high price." In 1852, he fell in love with a young Victoria Torres. Despite the fact that he was Jewish, they married in the Roman Catholic Church and raised their children in that faith. The couple moved to the small pueblo of Socorro, south of Albuquerque, where Nathan continued as a merchant and peddler.

Although he made a decent living in Socorro, the pueblo did not have the commercial advantages desired by Nathan. Better opportunities seemed to be waiting to the south, in Dona Ana County. Later he recalled the circumstances of the move:

> *Left Socorro and started with stock of goods for Dona Ana, N.M. There was some others who was to wait for me…[at] Fort Craig, so we be strong enough to go through the desert called Jornada del Muerto the distance… about 80 miles. When I reached now called Fort Craig formerly Cristobal the party gone and there I was all alone with my men teams & merchandise. Had not gone fore [far] found that the people had met with the Mescalero Apaches and several killed and wounded at a place called Mal-Paiz. I had to bury the dead and take care of the wounded before I started.*

Nathan secured a military escort for the remainder of the journey. He then embarked on a trek that took him west, to Tucson. What would become Arizona was then a part of the sprawling New Mexico Territory, extending from the Llano Estacado on the east to the Colorado River on the west. Appel traveled across southern Dona Ana County in 1856, but he was not impressed when he arrived in Tucson, then scarcely more than a rude adobe village without much to recommend it to an ambitious merchant. He turned back around to settle in Las Cruces along the Rio Grande. His family joined him there, and two years later they relocated to nearby Mesilla, where he became a naturalized American citizen. In partnership with trader Charles A. Hoppin, he opened a dramshop. Hoppin and Appel soon enlarged their business to include dry goods and wagon freighting. In pursuit of these ventures, Nathan once again visited southern Arizona. This time he got word of a silver mining boom in the region and decided to give Tucson another try.

Nathan later claimed that when his westward bound wagon train arrived at Stein's Pass in the Peloncillo Mountains of southwestern New Mexico, he encountered Indian Agent Dr. Michael Steck encamped with a large number

Nathan Benjamin Appel, Arizona's first identified Jewish settler, arrived in the late 1850s. Shown here in middle age. *Courtesy Arizona State Library, Archives and Public Records, History and Archives Division, #97-6453, Phoenix.*

of Apaches. The Apaches refused to allow Nathan to water his animals, so he appealed to Steck to intervene. The agent refused, and Nathan thereupon took matters into his own hands, posting armed teamsters and herders at the spring. He then led the animals, one by one, to the water. No bloodshed ensued, and the rest of the journey was uneventful.

By 1858, Nathan had opened a Tucson branch of Hoppin & Appel, followed by one in Tubac, an old Spanish settlement on the Santa Cruz River about fifty miles to the south. At the latter location, his general store conducted an extensive trade with Charles D. Poston's Sonora Exploring and Mining Company. Poston had a number of silver mines to the east and west of his Tubac headquarters. In addition, Hoppin and Appel did business with Sylvester Mowry's Patagonia silver mine southeast of Tubac and maintained a wagon freighting operation between the Rio Grande valley and Tucson. The 1860 census listed Nathan as living in Tubac with real and personal property valued at $6,500.

The outbreak of the Civil War changed Nathan's fortunes, but not for the better. The army withdrew its garrisons, disrupting wagon freighting and stagecoach service. Apache raiding increased, and settlements, including Tubac, were abandoned. Within a short time, only Tucson and Mowry's heavily fortified mine at Patagonia remained occupied.

An ardent Unionist, Nathan dissolved the partnership with Hoppin, a known Confederate sympathizer. He now had to go it alone. The owners of the Santa Rita Mine northwest of Tubac contracted with him to remove machinery from the abandoned works. He and his workmen made two trips to and from the Santa Rita, but on the third they were ambushed. Although no one was killed or seriously wounded, the raiders took sixty mules and one horse, effectively ending Appel's ability to move any more equipment. Word of approaching Confederate cavalry caused him to relocate to Mexico. The Appels settled just across the border in Sonora. There Nathan resumed merchandising on a limited scale, supplying local residents with what journalist J. Ross Browne described as "mescal and a few dry goods and trinkets."

Nathan Appel's first ventures in Arizona included a store in Tubac, shown here about a decade after he relocated permanently to Tucson. *From J. Ross Browne,* Adventures in the Apache Country, *1871.*

When he could, Nathan joined the large convoys of the major freighting companies on the road to Tucson. On one trip, he was traveling with freighters hauling merchandise up from Sonora when they were attacked by Apaches. A pitched battle ensued until the freighters ran out of ammunition and fled, leaving their wagons to be pillaged. Two teamsters and some women and children accompanying the train were killed. Nathan suffered minor wounds.

When Union forces from California chased the Confederates from the southern New Mexico Territory and reestablished some semblance of order, Nathan and his family returned to the United States. He reopened his general stores in Tubac and Tucson along with the wagon freighting business. Then Nathan entered politics.

In February 1863, President Lincoln signed the Organic Act, creating Arizona as a territory separate from New Mexico. In July of the following year, an election was held for the First Territorial Legislature. Nathan won a seat as a representative from southern Arizona in the lower house. The legislators met in the new capital of Prescott in the territory's mountainous north-central region. Nathan combined business with his public service, bringing some fifteen thousand pounds of flour from Sonora with him, which he readily sold. The legislature wrote a law code, created counties and authorized a militia to combat the Apaches. He participated actively in drafting bills, debating proposed laws and chairing the Committee on Enrolled and Engrossed Bills. When the session ended, however, he chose not to seek reelection and returned to Tucson, his family and business.

In the late 1860s, Nathan became embroiled in disputes in both Sonora and Arizona. During the Civil War, he had maintained friendly relations with the Mexicans, but this amicable situation deteriorated when the war between conservative allies of French-backed Emperor Maximilian I and the liberal government of Benito Juárez reached Sonora. In March 1866, Nathan had the misfortune to be transacting business in Magdalena when some imperial troops occupied the town. The commander demanded a "loan" of $250 in American currency. Nathan protested this extortion and refused to pay. He stated that as a citizen of the United States he could not be compelled to make such a loan. Furthermore, he was in Sonora representing a third party and did not have the money on his person. Unimpressed, the Mexicans threw Nathan in jail for a few days, confiscated his horse and forced the luckless merchant to do sentry duty. On his release, he dashed off a letter to the commander of the U.S. Army's Department of the Pacific at San Francisco, protesting this outrage and demanding that something be done to protect Americans in Mexico. But his effort went for naught. The letter made its way through military channels, finally being referred to the State Department in 1869, which did not act on the matter for another three years. State dismissed his complaint. By that time, however, Maximilian was dead, the French were gone, the conservatives had been suppressed and Nathan had given up on business in Mexico.

He was more successful in his legal battle with Sylvester Mowry. The disagreement arose over Mowry's demand for recovery of mining and other equipment allegedly left at the Patagonia Mine under Nathan's care during the early 1860s. At the same time, Nathan brought suit for payment of a long-standing debt owed to his Tubac store. When the legal dust settled, Nathan emerged victorious. The court dismissed the claim against him, upheld his claim against Mowry and ordered Mowry to pay court costs.

Nathan served as a deputy sheriff in Tucson for a time during the 1870s before returning to wagon freighting. In the following decade, however, the Arizona he had come to know began changing. The Southern Pacific Railroad, building east from Yuma, signaled the beginning of the end for large freighters like Nathan. But rather than retiring from the business, Nathan relocated to the town of Wilcox on the Southern Pacific mainline east of Tucson. From this location, his wagons served the developing Gila

River valley, the San Carlos Indian Reservation, the U.S. Army's post at Fort Thomas and the copper mines of the Globe district.

In 1883, Nathan quit wagon freighting for the last time. He had reached an age when many men contemplated retirement, but by no means was he ready to embark on a life of inactivity. He returned to Tucson law enforcement, joining the police department. His duties ranged from routine street patrols to serving as acting chief of the department. He made a number of arrests, primarily for drunk and disorderly conduct and opium smoking.

Sometimes Nathan was a bit too zealous when enforcing the law. A case in point: soon after joining the force, he arrested two young brothers from Globe who had come to Tucson looking for work and had set up camp in a lumberyard. Rousting the pair from their bedrolls at three o'clock in the morning, he kicked them in the ribs, drew his pistol and marched them off to jail. Nathan then prematurely announced to the newspapers that he had apprehended two dangerous army deserters. The military, however, proved the lads were not the deserters. They were released after paying a seven-dollar trespass fine, much to Nathan's chagrin.

On other occasions, however, his actions had a more positive outcome. While walking his beat one morning, he was stopped by a young man who reminded him that he had taken him in for smoking opium. After serving his sentence, the young man quit opium, moved to Los Angeles and got a job. He told Nathan that he was now drug-free, healthy and prosperous, and he owed it all to the policeman who arrested him that day.

Marital difficulties occasioned a move to California in 1887. The couple had separated, with Victoria and their daughters settling in Nogales, Arizona, and Nathan and his sons arriving in Los Angeles. Nathan obtained a position on the police force. He patrolled the crowded platforms of Southern Pacific's River Passenger Station and later its massive Arcade Depot, keeping order, pinching pickpockets and dispensing useful information to travelers. In 1890, Nathan was made bailiff of the police court.

Nathan was still serving as bailiff when he died on January 5, 1901, at the age of seventy-three. He received an impressive Masonic funeral, with much of the Los Angeles police force and several city officials in attendance. Presiding at the service was the Worshipful Master of Lodge No. 42, Abraham M. Edelman, son of the city's pioneer rabbi Abraham Wolf Edelman. A rabbi, perhaps the elder Edelman, also reportedly offered prayers over Appel's grave, something the free-thinking Nathan would have found ironic.

Alphonse Lazard, Arizona's Almost Forgotten Jewish Pioneer

Shortly after Appel opened his Tubac store, another Jew wandered into southern Arizona. Less well known today, Alphonse Lazard was born in the Alsace region of France in 1831. He left his homeland as a young man, journeyed about Europe and came to the United States in 1852. His cousins had established the house of Lazard Freres, a dry goods, banking and currency exchange businesses, originally in New Orleans, but later with offices in San Francisco and New York. Alphonse first worked in the firm's New York office but soon decided to try his luck out west. His brother, Solomon Lazard, was already a prominent businessman and civic leader in Los Angeles, and it may have been that he planned to seek him out. Alphonse moved west and worked for a while for a string of Indian trading posts in Nebraska, Kansas and Colorado. He traveled through New Mexico but did not make it to California. Rather he stopped in Tucson in 1859, and there he remained.

Alphonse soon became known around the Old Pueblo as "Frenchy" and entered into a butcher business with Sam Hughes and Hiram Stevens. When the Civil War broke out, Hughes, a staunch Unionist, decided to leave town. He left the butcher shop and other interests in the hands of his partners, who looked after them. Upon his return, Hughes rewarded Frenchy with property, launching his business career. Hughes also participated in a number of commercial ventures with Lazard during the 1860s and 1870s. Frenchy finally did get to Los Angeles in 1864 and briefly became a partner with his brother in a dry goods business. When that did not work out, he made his way back to southern Arizona.

Over the next two decades, Lazard operated freight wagons between New Mexico and Tucson. His trains occasionally fell prey to Apache raiders, costing both the lives of teamsters and expensive merchandise. In 1869, he established a timber and sawmill operation in the Santa Rita Mountains and hoped to supply the town with lumber for construction of "modern" frame buildings to replace the traditional, but out-of-date, adobe structures. An Indian attack the following year destroyed the mill, but Frenchy replaced it and became a builder and dry goods merchant in Tucson during the 1870s. Many of the town's first frame buildings were constructed by Lazard himself of lumber from his mill. Later he sold out his business and became one of the incorporators of Tucson's first bank. He also dealt in mines and real estate and maintained a ranch near Camp Crittenden. Between

Alphonse "Frenchy" Lazard arrived in Tucson in the late 1850s. He became a prominent businessman and banker. *Courtesy Arizona Historical Society, #1807, Tucson, Arizona.*

1876 and 1878, Frenchy again moved, this time to Southern California, but illness compelled his return to Tucson's drier climate.

A dapper little man known for his drooping dark moustache, Gallic charm and a straw skimmer shading his head from the noonday sun, Frenchy was popular in Tucson, but he never married. He had a reputation for honesty in his business and personal transactions and gave liberally to local charities. Although many of his business associates were Jews, his name did not appear among the lists of those observing the High Holy Days or participating in other events with the Jewish community. By the early 1890s, his physical and mental condition had begun to deteriorate. He moved to San Francisco, where, in late 1894, he entered the French Hospital for an extended stay. The following March, he managed to steal and hide a pistol. When the staff was otherwise occupied, he shot himself. When the news of Frenchy's death reached Arizona, the local press expressed sadness and reminded their readers of the role he had played in the development of Tucson and the territory. The Arizona Pioneers Historical Society, of which he was a member, wrote in memoriam of the little Frenchman:

> *The death of Alphonse Lazard deminishes* [sic] *the number of that brave and manly band that ventured on the frontier faced its dangers, understood its toils and experienced its privations. It is but just to him who was imbued with pride at the part he took in the early settlement and primary building up of the Territory that we should give recognition to the qualities he possessed: plainness and directness, physical and moral courage, honesty, generosity and charity.*

GOLDWATERS LEAD THE WAY

In 1858, a placer gold strike along the Gila River in southwestern Arizona about twenty miles upstream from the confluence with the Colorado River brought a rush of prospectors. They established Gila City as the center of the new district. Close on their heels were merchants from California, among them Jews, who, according to writer J. Ross Browne, came "with ready made clothing and fancy wares" to sell to the miners. While clothing was likely in demand, the residents of the hardscrabble town would have had little use for fancy wares. Boots, tools, picks and shovels and groceries proved far more saleable.

Nathan Appel stopped by Gila City to see what the excitement was all about but did not stay. Nathan Level, a Jewish shopkeeper who had emigrated from France, was there, as was fellow Frenchman Isaac Blum. Another Jewish visitor to the camp who would have a major effect on the development of Arizona was a peddler, Michel Goldwater.

Michel Goldwater was born in 1821 in Posen, part of Poland controlled by Russia. As a young man, he left his homeland, where life for Jews was becoming increasingly difficult. Michel, accompanied by his younger brother, Joe, headed to more liberal western Europe and separated. Michel found his way to Paris and then London, where he became a tailor, learned English and did well. He cut a dashing figure about town. Standing over six feet, he possessed a muscular build, fair hair and complexion and was always immaculately dressed. Soon he caught the eye of young Sarah Nathan, who came from a well-to-do family. The attraction was mutual. The two married in London's Great Synagogue and settled into a comfortable middle-class life. They welcomed their first child in late 1850 and were expecting their second when Joe showed up in 1851.

The younger Goldwater bore little resemblance to his brother, with a slight build, dark hair and more olive complexion. He had been knocking about Europe and brought with him tales of fortunes being made in the California gold fields. Much to Sarah's dismay, Joe's stories intrigued Michel. The same wanderlust and yearning for freedom that had led them from their homeland now beckoned them to the new world.

In 1852, the Goldwater brothers purchased steerage tickets to America. After three weeks of rough seas, cramped, smelly quarters and bad food, their packet arrived in New York. They journeyed on to San Francisco via Central America. The brothers arrived in the Mother Lode boomtown of Sonora in early 1853. It would be the first of many rough locations where

Left: Michel "Big Mike" Goldwater came to Arizona as a wagon peddler. He went on to establish a mercantile dynasty in the territory and state. *Courtesy Arizona Jewish Historical Society, Phoenix, Arizona.*

Right: Although Joseph Goldwater differed in appearance and temperament from his older brother, he knew how to keep his wits about him in a dangerous situation. *Courtesy Distinctive Collections, #BMG-AMP-004, Arizona State University Library, Tempe, Arizona.*

Michel and Joe sought their fortunes. They opened a saloon—a sure-fire moneymaker—on the first floor of a two-story wooden building. One of Sonora's many brothels occupied the second floor. While the brothers had nothing to do officially with the goings-on upstairs, the girls' presence brought in many a thirsty miner.

Once established in Sonora, Michel sent for Sarah and the children. The arrival of Michel's family strained the relationship between the brothers. Sarah had never liked Joe, blaming him for her husband's abrupt departure and separation. It was not long before Joe decamped to the northern California mining town of Shasta, where he set up a general store. Even with Joe gone, within a short time Sarah had had enough of the rough life. With the children, who now numbered three with a fourth on the way, she left for San Francisco. The city was no London, but it had a higher level of sophistication than Sonora.

To add to his troubles, Michel began having financial difficulties. By the late 1850s, the boom times of the California gold rush had definitely slowed. Fewer and fewer customers came into the saloon, and when they did, they were no longer prospectors on a spree, flashing gold nuggets and happy to buy everyone a drink. Customers still drank, just not as much or as frequently. Michel soon faced a declining income and mounting debts. Joe, on the other hand, had moved to Los Angeles and seemed to be doing surprisingly well. Michel shuttered the saloon and informed Sarah that he, too, would be moving to Los Angeles.

The Goldwater brothers came together once again in the dusty cowtown of Los Angeles. Still a community of adobes and rude wooden buildings, it possessed few amenities, having just one accommodation worthy of being called a hotel—the two-story Bella Union. There Michel found employment doing what he knew best, managing the billiard parlor and bar. Joe already operated a tobacco stand in the Bella Union. Sarah and the children joined Michel, and life was good.

Eventually, however, Michel's debts again caught up with him. He did not have the income to pay the lingering bills from the Sonora saloon. About this time, he heard of the strike at Gila City just across the Colorado River in the far southwest corner of New Mexico Territory. It seemed to offer a chance for a peddler to make a tidy sum. He convinced Joe—who needed little convincing when it came to adventurous schemes—to advance him the money for a wagon and inventory. He then set out in the heat of summer for the lower Gila and Colorado Rivers. In shacks, tents, lean-tos and sometimes in the shade of his own wagon, Michel sold tools, mining implements, clothing, provisions and "yankee notions" to prospectors eager to pay with gold dust and nuggets. The Goldwater association with Arizona had begun.

Joe bought goods for his brother's peddling in San Francisco on credit. Unfortunately, he signed "demand notes" allowing creditors to force immediate payment at any time. One individual chose to be hard-nosed and presented Joe with the demand. When the younger Goldwater could not come up with the money, other wholesalers became nervous and requested full payment as well. Almost overnight, the Goldwaters' small trading empire collapsed. In December 1862, all of their goods, as well as the peddler's wagon and mules, were sold at public auction.

Soon after the bankruptcy sale, Joe left for San Francisco seeking a new start. Michel, on the other hand, decided to remain in Southern California. Sarah and his growing family were now established in Los

Angeles. It proved to be a wise decision. Michel joined the Masonic lodge, and in a fortunate turn of events, one of his lodge brothers, merchant Bernard Cohn, presented him with an opportunity for employment and adventure.

The Town of Peace, Arizona's First Jewish "Community"

A Jew from Prussian Poland, Bernard Cohn had become a prosperous wool broker and real estate dealer in Los Angeles. He was active in both the Masons and the Jewish community, serving as president of Congregation Beth El in 1861. The following year, he received a letter describing the richness of the diggings at La Paz (The Peace), a settlement on the Colorado River. That letter, along with newspaper accounts of the money to be made selling provisions to the miners, prompted Cohn to brave the summer heat and lead a pack train with supplies from Los Angeles. By August 20, 1862, he had returned to LA with a sack containing, "about twenty pounds of the lumps or nuggets, found so plenty in those placers."

Profitable trading journeys convinced Cohn to establish a permanent store at La Paz. Since he did not intend to take up residence full-time along the Colorado, Cohn needed a clerk to staff the new venture. He asked Michel if he was interested. Goldwater was a logical choice. He had business experience (not always successful) and spoke perfect English, with a smattering of Spanish as well. He was used to the rough-and-tumble life of the mining town, and his tall, muscular frame would intimidate most of the characters that populated La Paz. Michel was broke, with a family to support, and by early 1863, he and his new employer had set up the store.

The ramshackle frontier settlement where Bernard Cohn and Michel Goldwater hoped to make their fortunes boasted a population of a little over three hundred. The heat in summer was scorching, and in winter, cold desert winds made the nights quite uncomfortable. Prospectors were scattered up and down along the Colorado, and in the nearby hills and washes, with more coming all the time. La Paz sprawled along the eastern riverbank. Business houses and accommodations ranged from a blanket on the ground to lean-tos and huts fashioned from the willows and other bushes growing along the river. Eventually, adobe buildings lined its main street. Other streets and alleys ran askew. One observer noted, "If laid out properly on a map, the

By the end of the nineteenth century, Arizona's first boomtown, La Paz, had become a collection of adobe ruins. *Courtesy Arizona Historical Society, #15347, Tucson, Arizona.*

town would have resembled...a cobweb drawn and blotted by a young child on a rumpled piece of paper."

A short time after Michel Goldwater, Isaac Goldberg also arrived at La Paz. Born in Russian Poland about 1836, he immigrated to California at age eighteen, eventually settling with his older brother Hyman, a storekeeper in San Bernardino. In the early 1860s, San Bernardino was the starting point of the trail to La Paz, and the Goldbergs heard plenty of stories about the opportunities for quick wealth along the Colorado River. Isaac undertook a trading venture there in 1863, later recalling that he sold not only all the goods he brought but the boxes in which the merchandise had traveled as well, so desperate for lumber were the inhabitants of La Paz.

At La Paz, Isaac joined his brother-in-law Philip Drachman, who also hailed from Russian Poland. He sailed to the United States on the same packet boat as the Goldwater brothers. They must have met, but instead of going on to California with his new acquaintances, Philip stayed in the east for a while to pursue a career as a tailor. It was not long, however, until he realized that the needle trade could not compare with the fortunes to be made out west. In 1854, he packed his bag and headed for the Golden State. There he met up with his younger sister Augusta, a pioneering woman who already had made her way to Southern California, where she married

Hyman Goldberg in 1852. Philip joined the Goldbergs at the La Paz store. Isaac and Philip staffed the counter (such as it was) and saw to the warehouse. Hyman, in San Bernardino, purchased and forwarded the merchandise to the Colorado. This arrangement worked well, and the store prospered.

Heyman Mannasse, who also had emigrated from Russian Poland, arrived on the Colorado with a cattle drive in late 1863. His so-called Variety Store at La Paz sold goods needed by the miners along with a few luxuries, such as soap, silk shirts, fine wines and liquors and some gourmet food items. Within a year, Heyman's net worth was estimated at $2,000, a tidy sum in those days.

Philip Drachman, an early settler at La Paz, later went to Tucson and established a general store there. *Courtesy Arizona State Library, Archives and Public Records, History and Archives Division, #97-8231, Phoenix.*

Two other Jewish merchants destined to play prominent roles in Arizona also settled at La Paz. Benjamin Block, a native of Alsace-Lorraine, appeared along the Colorado River in the late fall of 1862. He had failed in a livery stable business in San Luis Obispo, California, and the La Paz boom offered a chance to recoup his losses. Block's younger cousin Michael Wormser came to the United States from Moselle, France, in 1858. On his arrival, he worked for a while at menial jobs in New York before Block paid his passage to California. He had been Block's partner in the ill-fated livery, but after this venture, Wormser made a comfortable living in central California through peddling, horse trading and money lending. Unlike his cousin, he saw La Paz not as a place to start over but as an opportunity to increase the capital he had already accumulated. Both Mike Wormser and Ben Block were stout and balding, but there the resemblance ended. Block came across as gregarious, kind and easygoing, whereas Wormser was seen as contentious, suspicious and all business.

While most Jews who came to La Paz were merchants of one sort or another, Alexander Levin, born in Prussia in 1834, pursued a different line. His Pioneer Brewery and Saloon offered refreshment to the parched community. The beer may have been of questionable quality, but it was nonetheless welcome, as were the other drinkables that Levin kept behind the bar. The enterprising publican also saw to the personal hygiene of his customers by operating a public bathhouse. It featured a novel "shower bath" where the grimy prospector or traveler could rinse off the desert dust before heading into the Pioneer for a drink.

By the close of 1863, La Paz could boast a small but active and mostly prospering Jewish community, with Michel Goldwater, Big Mike or just Mike, in the forefront. Goldwater's hard work at the La Paz store paid off when he graduated from Cohn's employee to a full partner in the firm. Their business, along with that of the other merchants, expanded greatly with the discovery of rich gold deposits in the Bradshaw Mountains of central Arizona. The Colorado River camp was transformed almost overnight into the principal port of entry for the bonanza. Rather than being depopulated as prospectors left for the new diggings, La Paz now bustled with teamsters, muleskinners, rivermen and transients. Newly arrived stagecoach and steamboat passengers gathered up their baggage and raced to catch transportation to the mines. Merchants stood in the doorways of their warehouses eager to receive merchandise they would either offer for sale in their stores or, more likely, forward on to the interior mining camps.

In the early 1860s, travelers who called at La Paz brought news of the secession of the Southern states, followed by the Civil War in the east. They also carried the welcome announcement of the formation, in February 1863, of the Territory of Arizona, separate from New Mexico. Although many residents considered La Paz as a possible territorial capital, that honor went in 1864 to the new town of Prescott near the Bradshaw Mountains mining districts. Nevertheless, La Paz merchants saw that there was still money to be made, as the capital would have to be supplied, with most merchandise coming through their town. The presence of a territorial bureaucracy, along with the army's Fort Whipple located nearby and miners from the surrounding diggings, provided a substantial customer base. Soon wagon trains, traders and merchants were on the road from the Colorado.

The Late Herman Ehrenberg...Mike Goldwater Names a Town

The good times at La Paz lasted until 1867. In the interior, mining camps came and went, but the boom itself lingered. As Prescott grew, its citizens also provided a rising market for goods from the merchandise warehouses on the Colorado River. While the Colorado had given life to La Paz, it also caused its demise. Over the winter of 1866–67, the river flooded, this time changing its channel altogether. The result was that La Paz now stood

Above: View of the Colorado River port of Ehrenberg in the 1870s. Merchant warehouses line the bank. *Courtesy Arizona Jewish Historical Society, Phoenix, Arizona.*

Opposite: Even as a ruin at the turn of the twentieth century, the Goldwater warehouse in Ehrenberg was impressive. *Courtesy Arizona State Library, Archives and Public Records, History and Archives Division, #96-3095, Phoenix.*

high and dry, some six miles from the water. While optimists continued to promote the location as the gateway to Arizona, within a year, businessmen were looking for a better port.

Mike Goldwater led the exodus from La Paz, finding a more suitable location a few miles downriver at Mineral City. He renamed the spot Ehrenberg in honor of his friend and mining engineer Herman Ehrenberg, a non-Jew who had been murdered at the Dos Palmas stage stop. At the new town, Goldwater built a substantial warehouse, said to be the largest in the territory. With thick adobe walls, it measured seventy-five by one hundred feet. Inside, his son Morris kept track of an extensive stock of merchandise for the company's wholesale dry goods operation as well as freight awaiting transport to central Arizona. One by one, other merchants followed, and La Paz entered into an irreversible decline.

About the time of the move to Ehrenberg, Mike Goldwater's business relationship with Bernard Cohn ended. Their new store and forwarding business was prospering, but Cohn had tired of Arizona and wanted to concentrate on his Southern California interests. Big Mike, on the other hand, saw Arizona as full of business opportunities. He and Cohn parted on good terms. Back in Southern California, Cohn became a partner in the wholesale grocery business of Hellman, Haas & Company. He served on the Los Angeles City Council in the 1870s and 1880s and during this time added to the town gossip by maintaining two families, one Jewish and the other Mexican Catholic. Bernard Cohn died in Los Angeles in 1889.

With Cohn's departure, Mike was on his own, but not for long. Brother Joe soon appeared. He had given up on business in California. After Joe's arrival, Mike sent Morris back to be with his mother and siblings in San Francisco, where he continued his education and practical training in business before rejoining his father and uncle.

In addition to the Ehrenberg warehouse, during the 1870s, Joe operated a branch store at Parker's Landing upstream from La Paz. There he supplied the Colorado River Indian Reservation, sold horses to the army, provided the army with carpentry and blacksmithing services and furnished local livestock herders with liquor and cigars. Freight teams from the Goldwaters' Ehrenberg headquarters, some capable of hauling over sixty thousand pounds of merchandise, became a common sight lumbering along the rough dirt roads and trails in western and central Arizona. Through the 1870s, the Goldwaters supplied interior communities, stored and shipped gold dust and nuggets for other merchants, acted as agents for the Arizona and New Mexico stage line between Ehrenberg and San Francisco and had the contract for transporting the mail between Mohave County and Yuma.

Down South at the Yuma Crossing

Located in the far southwestern portion of the territory, Yuma was one of the hottest and driest places in Arizona. But it had one advantage, the Colorado River. With the army's Fort Yuma on the California side, its quartermaster depot in Arizona, ferry service between the two, a major steamboat landing and the location in 1875 of the territorial prison, the settlement quickly developed into western Arizona's principal port of entry and commercial center. A German Jewish immigrant, Abe Frank, operated a popular general merchandise store in Yuma for a number of years. Frank arrived in Arizona around 1867. At first, he kept a store at La Paz but later followed Mike Goldwater to Ehrenberg. When the Goldwaters decided to dispose of their Ehrenberg forwarding and commission business in 1880, they sold the operation to Frank. His purchase briefly made him one of the most prominent businessmen in the territory. But just as Mike had anticipated, within a few years, railroads crossed Arizona, dealing a death blow to the large forwarding and commission companies. Private and government freight could now be shipped by rail, with smaller outfits handling transportation

Yuma in the 1870s. Despite the arrival of the Southern Pacific Railroad, Yuma remained largely an adobe town. *Courtesy Arizona State Library, Archives and Public Records, History and Archives Division, #98-7001, Phoenix.*

from trackside to customers. In 1883, Frank sold out and moved south to Yuma. In addition to storekeeping and some local freighting, Frank devoted much of his later life to politics and public service as a legislator, prison commissioner, mayor and a probate judge.

Abe Frank was not the only Jew to seek his fortune in Yuma. Prussian-born Julius Samter arrived in Yuma (at that time called Arizona City) in 1872. He became a general merchant, probably buying out the stock of an earlier storekeeper, Louis Landesberger. His successful Main Street stand soon became known as Samter's "Cheap Cash Store," and behind the counter could be found another Arizona pioneer, Hyman Goldberg, who had moved down from La Paz. Goldberg left when Samter expanded to Phoenix and Florence. Unfortunately, fire destroyed Samter's Yuma headquarters on the night of January 13, 1878. Although he struggled to keep the business going, by April, Samter's property had been sold and he had left Arizona.

"Black Ike" Levy

French Jew Isaac Levy had a long and colorful career in Yuma. Levy arrived in the 1870s having come from California by sea and steamboat up the Colorado. He found employment on the river, first as a steward on a steamboat, but soon worked his way up to master of the tow barge *Black Crook*. The vessel was named for a popular musical play in New York. The barge was 128 feet long by 28 feet wide and carried up to 100 tons of freight. Levy likely acquired the sobriquet "Black Ike" from his barge's name. Levy left the river business, and he became proprietor of the Colorado Hotel on Yuma's Gila Street. With Gallic flair, he touted the establishment as the "Best Hotel in Arizona," with a restaurant over which he gave his personal attention. And being French, the food of course would be *magnifique*. The hotel also had a bar (of course), and Levy assured the public that everything was first-class and would "meet the approbation of the resident and traveling public."

In late 1883, Levy partnered with an English Jew, Isaac Lyons, in a store at Clip, a steamboat landing and mill town about seventy miles upriver from Yuma. Lyons had a somewhat tarnished reputation due to his previous association with an old friend, Joe Goldwater. Allegedly, Joe purchased and shipped from San Francisco a large quantity of merchandise without paying. A U.S. marshal attempted to serve a warrant and seize the goods, but Goldwater and Lyons barred the door. A short standoff ensued when

"Black Ike" Levy captained a tow barge such as this one on the Colorado River in the 1870s. *Courtesy Arizona State Library, Archives and Public Records, History and Archives Division, #07-2066, Phoenix.*

the armed citizens of Yuma came to the aid of the popular Lyons and Goldwater. They defended the store until the two owners finally surrendered. Both went to jail for a short time, after which Joe returned to San Francisco to face yet another bankruptcy, and Lyons, his shelves stripped of inventory, had to start all over. Unfortunately, Lyons's bad luck followed him into the partnership with Ike Levy at Clip. The mine was not nearly as profitable as anticipated, and the store went bankrupt within a year. Levy rebounded from this disaster, returning to Yuma in the mid-1880s, selling general merchandise and investing in mines.

As for Isaac Lyons, his time in Arizona was shorter. He tried storekeeping again, but by 1891, he was dead. Levy then finally realized something positive from their association. He bought a couple acres of land from the estate on which he built a new store and a home for his family. He remained there until his death in 1899.

David Calisher, Firebug or Storekeeper?

In the late 1880s, David Calisher appeared in Yuma and opened a general merchandise store. He came from Tombstone under a cloud as a suspected arsonist. The son of merchant Martin Calisher, he had been accused of setting fire to his father's general store and lumber business in 1882 for the insurance money. Although indicted, he was acquitted. Nevertheless, sentiment in Tombstone ran high against him. David realized that he probably ought to get out of town fast. This led to a hasty departure and eventual arrival in Yuma. There he prospered, with no hint of scandal for the remainder of his long career.

After 1900, the small business community of Yuma expanded as the town's focus shifted from the river trade and railroad to being a center for the developing irrigated agriculture in southwestern Arizona and southeastern California. A number of Jewish merchants opened stores in Yuma during this period. Among these were Harry Brownstetter and George Michaelson, proprietors of the New York Store, which sold dry goods and clothing; two other dry goods merchandisers, Herman and Sol Goldsmith; Charles Mandelbaum, a confectioner and tobacconist; Edward Frankel, a jeweler; and M.B. Goldstein, a dealer in secondhand goods. Although not all of these shopkeepers remained long in Yuma, a few, such as the Goldsmiths, continued to operate their stores well into the twentieth century.

2

GOLD RUSH MERCHANTS

TREASURE IN THE HILLS

Michael Wormser came to Arizona for one reason: to make money and return to his homeland a wealthy man. He had no love for the land of the Apaches, cacti, rattlesnakes and scorpions. It was dangerous and uncomfortable. The store he and partner Ben Block operated at La Paz did well enough, but it was not the moneymaker he had hoped for. From prospectors he heard reports of fortunes being made in the Bradshaw Mountains to the east. Chunks of gold the size of potatoes lay scattered about just for the taking. In early 1863, therefore, he left Block at the La Paz store and headed for the hills. Much to his disappointment, however, Wormser soon found that the tales of quick riches had become exaggerated with each telling. There was still money to be made in the central mines, but it would require hard work, not just a stroll picking up nuggets.

Wormser did work hard, but mineral wealth eluded him. He tired of prospecting and turned to what he knew best—business. He brought supplies from La Paz and opened a dry goods store at Weaver, a camp along Weaver Creek. The deposits at Weaver had attracted miners from California and Mexico, and the store did a brisk trade. After one season, however, the easily retrievable placer gold began running out, and the prospectors started looking elsewhere. Seeking to keep up with his customers, Wormser closed out at Weaver and moved on to the new camp of Walker along Lynx Creek. From a log shack, he sold what merchandise he could get Block to ship him,

M. WORMSER.

Stout and humorless, Michael Wormser came to Arizona to make a fortune—and he did.
Author's collection.

but his tenure there also was brief, as declining placers and trouble with local Yavapai Indians drove most of the miners away.

Wormser stuck it out at Walker through late 1864. By that time, the territorial capital at Prescott had been established. Although the new community had plenty of saloons to slake the thirst of miners, politicians and soldiers, it lacked places to buy things and things to buy. Initially, La Paz traders, such as the Goldwaters, sent wagon and mule trains with merchandise to sell, but the road between La Paz and Prescott was arduous and hazardous. The frequency of deliveries depended on when the goods arrived from California and could be interrupted by bad weather or Indian attacks. Quality, variety and price also differed from shipment to shipment, depending on what the wholesalers and forwarders could obtain. Nevertheless, the arrival of the wagon trains touched off celebrations in Prescott as the eager citizenry snapped up whatever the freighters had to sell.

Such a state of affairs could not continue for long. The territorial capital needed outlets that sold goods at fairly stable prices and warehouses to store merchandise to avoid shortages. Wormser recognized this need and built an adobe store and warehouse on the corner of Montezuma and Goodwin Streets. It was the first commercial building fronting the as yet empty town square. There he sold a variety of mining and domestic goods, canned food, clothing, liquor and even livestock. The store was known as Wormser & Company, for by that time Michael and Ben Block had taken on two partners, German immigrant Henry Wunderlich and Aaron Wertheimer, a thirty-three-year-old Jew from the Duchy of Baden. Wunderlich would not stay with the firm for long, but Wertheimer remained until his death ten years later.

In 1870, Ben Block left Wormser & Company for the Salt River valley. The Prescott firm now became Wormser & Wertheimer. While Wertheimer served as the firm's agent in Arizona and California, Wormser maintained the store. By this time, he had acquired a reputation as an irascible introvert and had few, if any, friends. He spent more and more of his time in court, either suing those whom he felt had slighted him monetarily or defending himself against similar lawsuits. Aaron Wertheimer, on the other hand, was pleasant and outgoing and became the perfect front man, much as Ben Block had been. He traveled about the territory and California, making friends wherever he went, contracting and drumming up business for the company. This arrangement worked quite well, and Wormser & Wertheimer became Prescott's leading commercial house in the early 1870s.

Wertheimer's sudden passing in January 1874, however, ended not only the partnership but Wormser's prosperity as well. Suppliers and customers

SOL BARTH

Sol Barth, probably Arizona's most colorful Jewish pioneer. *Courtesy Arizona Jewish Historical Society, Phoenix, Arizona.*

accustomed to dealing with the affable Wertheimer found their relations with the dour and contentious Wormser strained. Declining retail sales, pressure from California wholesalers and a series of bad accounts that had no legal remedy forced him to sell his mercantile and real estate holdings and start over in the Salt River valley.

Other Jewish merchants doing business in central Arizona in the 1860s included Heyman Mannasse, who appeared in Prescott shortly after Wormser, as well as Mike Goldwater. Initially, Big Mike did not take a major stake in the new capital or nearby gold diggings. He preferred to stay in La Paz and Ehrenberg, tending his store and forwarding goods to other merchants. He did, however, make a deal to supply two young and ambitious Jews, Sol Barth and Aaron Barnett, with dry goods and liquor to sell in the interior mining districts for a portion of the profits.

Sol Barth's origins are somewhat obscure. Some claim that he was born in the United States of parents who had emigrated from Posen but returned to their homeland when Barth was an infant. The more commonly accepted story has Barth being born in Posen and immigrating to the United States when barely a teenager. In the company of an uncle who had converted to Mormonism, he traveled to Michigan and then to Utah. He did not adopt his uncle's faith, nor did he stay in Utah long, moving on to seek his fortune in California. There he was reported to have driven a freight team from Southern California to Tucson and back. In Los Angeles, Barth met and became an employee of Mike Goldwater, who quickly had him working on the Colorado, first at a trading post at Fort Mojave and then at Cohn and Goldwater's La Paz store and warehouse. Aaron Barnett was a young French Jew who came to California looking for excitement as well as riches and wound up along the Colorado River. Perhaps it was Barnett's skill at playing the banjo or his pleasing manner that first caused Mike Goldwater to notice him. Whatever the reason, teaming Barth and Barnett together was a good move. The trading venture proved quite profitable, and with Goldwater's backing, the two went on to establish the third dry goods store in the territorial capital.

Prescott Grows Up

As merchants put down roots in Prescott and opened permanent stores, the days of limited supplies and fluctuating prices became a thing of the past. While the arrival of freight trains still stirred excitement, customers no longer had to scramble to buy merchandise from the back of a wagon. Better business connections with the Pacific coast and improved transportation routes from the Colorado River enabled storekeepers to offer a broader and fairly consistent inventory. Groceries, liquors, medicines, clothing, boots, shoes, firearms and ammunition, housewares and hardware were displayed in long glass cabinets and on floor-to-ceiling shelves. An increasing number of settlers brought their families to Prescott, and store inventories expanded and became more sophisticated. By the end of the 1860s, the hard work of Wormser & Company, Barnett & Barth and the other merchants had endowed Prescott with an air of stability and permanence.

Storekeepers frequently sought other ways to supplement their incomes. Barth took a pack train east to trade at Zuni Pueblo in New Mexico and returned with a load of salt for sale in Prescott. Barnett & Barth also obtained the contract to carry the mail once a week between Prescott and Albuquerque and later had the service between Prescott, Tucson and Tubac. Occasionally, either Barth or Barnett would make the trip, but most of the time they hired riders. Besides their mail contracts, Barnett & Barth ran a type of express service, transporting gold from outlying mining camps to Prescott. It was in this line that Barth found himself mired in the first of many scandals. Over the summer of 1864, he reported that he had been robbed of a gold shipment while on the trail. His story, however, had some inconsistencies, and soon newspapers accused him of staging a "sham" robbery and lining his own pockets with the gold. Although there was not enough evidence to arrest him, the incident damaged Barth's reputation for some time. Four years later, a group of miners claimed to have uncovered a portion of the gold allegedly taken from Barth. By that time, however, the matter had been largely forgotten and Barth had moved on to other adventures.

During the 1870s, Prescott underwent slow but steady commercial growth despite the loss of the territorial capital to Tucson in 1867 and a decline in the importance of the military in central Arizona. The local economy improved over the summer of 1877 when two Jewish businessmen from San Francisco opened the town's first bank. Sol and Samuel Lewis were tobacco dealers by trade and likely did a little moneylending on the side. They had business connections in Prescott, and Sol saw that while some merchants

Above: David Levy and Company for many years sold general merchandise from a store on Prescott's "Whiskey Row." *Author's collection.*

Opposite: Interior of D. Levy and Company's Prescott store around the turn of the century. *Courtesy Sharlot Hall Museum Library and Archives, Prescott, Arizona.*

made loans, exchanged money and stored valuables in their safes, Prescott and the surrounding region needed a regular bank. The brothers, therefore, enlisted fellow San Franciscans Joseph May and Joseph Brandenstein and ex–Nevada general merchant Martin Kales, along with some local businessmen, in founding the Bank of Arizona. For all intents and purposes, Lewis and Kales ran the bank, with the former as president and the latter as cashier. The presence of a permanent financial institution allowed Prescott to retain some of its economic prestige.

As Prescott matured, established merchants vied with a host of new arrivals. Two eager young Polish Jews, brothers David and Abe Henderson,

had a thriving general merchandise business in Prescott in the late 1860s and 1870s. David spent most of his time in San Francisco making purchases for the store and keeping abreast of financial developments, while Abe took care of things in Arizona. The arrangement worked well until 1873, when the ambitious Hendersons decided that opportunities in the territory were too limited. Abe closed the store and joined his brother in San Francisco, where they established themselves as buying and shipping agents for Arizona companies.

In the same year that the Hendersons left Prescott, H. Asher & Company, another San Francisco–based concern, moved in and opened a dry goods store. The firm sent Hyman Ellis to manage the day-to-day operations of what soon became known as the San Francisco Store. Business was good, and by the end of 1875, H. Asher & Company had moved to a larger building and changed the store's name to the White House, still promising customers "fair and square dealing" in a wide variety of merchandise.

Hyman Ellis left H. Asher & Company in 1876 and moved to Phoenix. His departure left a vacancy that was filled by Louis Wollenberg (sometimes spelled Wollenburg), a German Jew who had immigrated to the United States in the 1850s. By 1860, he had moved to San Francisco and from there traded goods in mining camps in the Mother Lode and Nevada. With his arrival in Prescott, the store became known as Asher & Wollenberg, and it advertised in the *Arizona Miner* that it would sell dry goods at prices "Cheaper than the Cheapest." Despite this bold claim, the store soon closed and relocated to Phoenix.

Wollenberg, however, remained in Prescott and entered into a partnership with his brother, Marks, and Polish Jews Bennet Ellis (likely Hyman's cousin) and David Levy. Their store, B. Ellis & Company, lasted until 1879, when Ellis departed. The Wollenbergs then reorganized the partnership, opening a new general merchandise store under the name D. Levy & Company. This arrangement lasted almost three years, until Marks Wollenberg left to open his own store. Louis continued the business as one of Prescott's leading dry goods and grocery merchants into the twentieth century. D. Levy & Company also continued at a site adjacent to the Palace Saloon on Montezuma Street's Whiskey Row until well after the beginning of the twentieth century under the direction of David Levy's son, Nathan. Both Levy and Wollenberg became dealers in hides and wool as well. In addition, A. Blumberg's New York Store, Blumberg and Sam Dryer's Model Cash Grocery and Ben Silverman's tailor shop graced Montezuma Street during this period.

Goldwaters Finally Make the Move

Although Mike and Joe Goldwater had freighted goods and backed trading ventures to the central Arizona mines from the mid-1860s, the brothers themselves would be comparative latecomers to the region. Business at Ehrenberg was good, and they took a conservative stance, supplying stores in Prescott and keeping a close eye on business conditions. An unsuccessful venture in the Salt River valley in the early 1870s added to their reluctance to take on new projects. Eventually, however, Mike came to believe that Prescott might be ripe for a new store, and with the mines and retail trade along the Colorado in a seemingly irreversible decline, he decided to make the move. Mike arrived in Prescott in June 1876 and secured a lease for space in a substantial new brick building on the southeast corner of Cortez and Goodwin Streets. The Goldwaters kept the warehouse and shipping facilities at Ehrenberg for a few more years, but from 1876 until the twentieth century, Prescott would be their center of operations.

The store bore the name of J. Goldwater & Bro., but Joe initially remained in San Francisco to care for his seriously ill wife. In the meantime, Mike saw to the opening of the new store in October 1876. At first business was

The Goldwaters' second store in Prescott. The signs on the front and side indicate Morris and his brothers are taking over from their father. *Courtesy Distinctive Collections, BMG-AMP-008c, Arizona State University Library, Tempe, Arizona.*

slow. While the town was nice enough, and existing merchants did a steady business, it was difficult for a new store to gain a foothold. Nevertheless, Mike remained optimistic, and his optimism paid off as mining underwent a resurgence and the territorial capital returned to Prescott in 1877. Mike employed his sons Morris and Sam as clerks and Henry as manager of the Ehrenberg warehouse.

Over the ensuing decade, the Goldwaters' Prescott operation underwent a number of changes as commerce expanded. In 1879, Mike supervised construction of a new two-story brick building at Union and Cortez Streets to house the store on the ground floor and a Masonic hall on the second. The location opened in early 1880. Joe had returned to Prescott in 1879 but did not stay long. Now a widower, he seemed to have little interest in the business, and in May of the following year, J. Goldwater & Bro. dissolved with Joe taking his proceeds and striking out on his own. The new firm became M. Goldwater & Son, the son being Morris. With a slight build and dark hair and eyes, Morris took after his uncle Joe in appearance. He supplemented his receding hairline with a luxuriant mustache that drooped almost below his chin. Despite a fire that damaged the building soon after its opening, the store did well. With Morris taking

Morris Goldwater wearing his Masonic medals. Many Jews in early Arizona participated in fraternal organizations such as the Masons. *Courtesy Distinctive Collections, #BMG-AMP-006, Arizona State University Library, Tempe, Arizona.*

on increased responsibility in Prescott, Mike began spending more and more time in California. Early in 1887, he decided it was time to retire, ending the partnership and moving permanently to San Francisco, where he lived with Sarah until his death in 1903.

The torch now passed to a new generation as Morris assumed complete control of the Goldwater interests in central Arizona. With the sale of the Ehrenberg operation in 1880, Henry relocated to Prescott but left the firm four years later to pursue his dreams in Mexico and Yuma. Sam had opened his own small tobacco store. Their younger brother Baron joined the family business in 1882. Well-schooled in the retail trade, having worked at Wanamaker's department store in Philadelphia, Baron was diligent in his duties, and the house of M. Goldwater & Bro. prospered. Henry had little success in his undertakings away from Prescott, and in 1888 he returned to the firm, which became M. Goldwater & *Bros.*

By the 1880s, many merchants who had pioneered along the Colorado River and in the mountains of central Arizona had begun to see promise in Phoenix, and many chose to relocate or at least establish branch stores there. Prescott would remain important for local and regional business and as a pleasant mountain town where desert dwellers could escape the summer heat.

3

THE DESERT BLOOMS
IN THE SALT RIVER VALLEY

Aaron Barnett Takes a Chance

Southeast from Prescott, the Salt River emerges from its headwaters in the highlands of eastern Arizona and flows through a flat desert valley ringed by low mountains and studded with occasional rocky outcroppings or buttes. In ancient times, the Hohokam People had diverted water from the Salt River into a complex of canals and ditches to irrigate crops. Later, the Akimel O'Odam (Pima) People also irrigated valley fields of maize, beans and squash. In 1867, a group of disappointed miners from the mountains of central Arizona led by former Confederate soldier Jack Swilling cleaned out and re-excavated some of the old canals, routed water into the desert and began farming. The combination of water and rich alluvial soil resulted in successful harvests of wheat, barley and corn. By 1870, the residents had agreed on a townsite near the valley's center and named the location Phoenix. Despite its small size and rude appearance, early Phoenix attracted a sprinkling of Jewish settlers.

Aaron Barnett led the way. He may have decided to engage in some speculation in Phoenix as early as 1867, and his name appears as treasurer of the Swilling Irrigation and Canal Company. Over the summer of 1870, Barnett again was reported to be in Phoenix selling general merchandise from a wagon. The genial French banjo picker quickly became one of the most popular businessmen in town. That fall, he and partner Benjamin Block located a branch of their Wickenburg store in an adobe building on

Washington Street, Phoenix's main commercial street shortly after the town's founding. *Courtesy Arizona State Library, Archives and Public Records, History and Archives Division, #97-0965, Phoenix.*

Washington Street. Block took charge of the Phoenix operation, purveying a wide variety of merchandise, including groceries, clothing and farming supplies. Barnett and Block brought one of the first threshers in the valley to Phoenix in 1873.

STOREKEEPERS COME AND GO

Jews from other parts of Arizona soon followed Barnett and Block to the Salt River valley, where competition among merchants became intense. In addition, the financial panic of 1873 and subsequent depression resulted in a tightening of credit and a slump in agricultural prices, all of which pained valley merchants. For example, Heyman Mannasse, who had moved from Prescott to Wickenburg in the late 1860s, opened a Phoenix branch in 1872. He hired a young man by the name of S. Abrahamson to manage this store. Abrahamson quickly gained a reputation as one of the region's most progressive businessmen. Despite his efforts, problems with creditors and poor sales in the Wickenburg store, along with a decline in the farm trade, compelled Mannasse to close out his branch operation the following year. He kept the store in Wickenburg until his death there in 1875.

Mike Goldwater appeared in the Salt River valley with the idea of establishing a store and grain dealership. By November 1872, a stock of dry goods had been purchased from a failed merchant, and other merchandise had been shipped from Prescott. The following month, J. Goldwater & Bro. opened its doors. Morris had charge of the new store and actively promoted the business, going so far as to dedicate a space in the building for the federal government to use as a telegraph office. He even offered himself as telegrapher. Despite such innovative ventures, the depressed grain market and a lack of retail sales made the Phoenix store unprofitable. Mike decided to close up in the spring of 1875 to concentrate on operations at Ehrenberg and later Prescott.

There is an indication that Barnett and Block may have been forced to close as well. In December 1874, the partners disposed at auction some of their Phoenix townsite property. The money went to satisfy a judgement brought against them by creditors. Michael Wormser also encountered financial difficulties, and his business failed. Wormser would rebound from this loss to become a moneylender and the largest landowner south of the Salt River. Barnett and Block recouped their fortunes and turned their efforts to freighting in southern Arizona and Sonora.

The Goldmans Make It Big

Despite a gloomy business outlook in the mid-1870s, some merchants reasoned that with a railroad connection and proper water management, Phoenix could flourish. Among these hopefuls was Adolph Goldman. Goldman was born in the Palatinate of southwestern Germany in 1848. His father had been a well-to-do farmer, but after his death, the family's resources reached such a low state that the older sons, Adolph and Charles, had to leave home. Instead of just looking for jobs in the vicinity, the brothers made their way to California. Adolph clerked in a store and learned English and the retail trade before moving to Virginia City, Nevada. There he set up a tobacco stand, but a penchant for gambling led him to the brink of financial ruin. After too many bad runs at the gaming tables, he took what little money he had left and moved to Arizona. Charles had been in the territory since 1871 and was employed in Prescott as a clerk for the mercantile house of C.P. Head and Co. Adolph chose to settle in Phoenix and found work as a

The Goldman brothers—Leo, Adolph and Charles—prominent Phoenix merchants during the late nineteenth century. *Courtesy Arizona Jewish Historical Society, Phoenix, Arizona.*

clerk, bookkeeper for Wormser and Wertheimer. He later became a teamster for Barnett and Block, driving trains of monstrous wagons filled with barley from Phoenix to Fort Mohave.

After Barnett and Block closed, Adolph decided that riding a jerky wagon and cracking his whip all day in the desert sun, while keeping an eye out for Indians and bandits, was not the career for him. Storekeeping was more his line, and whereas his former employers had made some bad business decisions, he would learn from their mistakes and prosper. On a return trip to the Salt River valley, therefore, he stopped in Prescott and obtained backing from C.P. Head (probably through the good offices of his brother) for a general merchandise store. He opened in 1875 in the rundown adobe building on Washington Street. His principal competitor was Miguel Peralta, who had a prime location at the corner of Central and Washington Streets. But Peralta also had a gambling habit, and Adolph

The Goldman store in Phoenix. The top of the façade shows 1874 as its founding date. *Courtesy Arizona Jewish Historical Society, Phoenix, Arizona.*

knew what that could lead to. He bided his time, and when Peralta's losses caused him to go broke, Adolph purchased the store along with other of Peralta's holdings and moved in his own merchandise. He was joined by Charles, who had left C.P. Head in 1876 to become a country merchant serving the cattle ranchers and farmers in the Williamson valley near Prescott. His brother's success, however, prompted him to close out and move to Phoenix. Their younger brother Leo arrived soon after, and together they formed the general merchandise house of Goldman & Company. Charles bought out Adolph's interest in the firm in 1879. Adolph returned to Germany while Charles and Leo remained and became two of the Salt River valley's leading merchants.

Seeking new sales opportunities, Goldman & Company expanded to the mining camps east of Phoenix. As early as January 1879, Leo had established a general store in the silver camp of Picket Post (later called Pinal City). This store also served outlying mines and smelters. When the smelters consolidated at Butte, the Goldmans built a substantial adobe store there under the management of Gus Hirschfeld. The year 1882 proved to be the most successful time at both Pinal City and Butte. The Goldmans' stores kept busy supplying a steady stream of prospectors, laborers, ranchers and soldiers. A serious decline in production at the area's leading mine, the Silver King, the following year, however, caused business at Pinal City to become "sluggish." The Goldmans closed out, deciding to concentrate on the Butte store. This decision also proved unfortunate, and when the Butte mill closed in 1884, they gave up and shipped their inventory back to Phoenix.

Hyman Goldberg and the Hazards of Arizona Business

Pioneer merchant Hyman Goldberg, who had been storekeeping along the Colorado River since the mid-1860s, arrived in Phoenix with his son Aaron in June 1875. In town to establish a branch for Yuma businessman Julius Samter, the Goldbergs opened the store on Washington Street. Their newspaper advertising used the tried-and-true slogan "Quick Sales and Small Profits." The profits turned out to be smaller than expected, and in 1877, Hyman left town to open a store in Florence in Pinal County. Aaron remained in Phoenix, leaving Samter's employ and launching his own general store. Unsuccessful in Florence, Hyman returned to the Salt River valley in 1878. He went back to work for Samter, but things did not go well for the elder Goldberg. Old debts caught up with him, and that year he was judged to be bankrupt. Aaron, on the other hand, had been doing quite well for himself. In 1879, he took his father into the business, which became known as H. Goldberg & Son.

In addition to the Phoenix store, H. Goldberg & Son had a branch in Harshaw, a silver mining boomtown in southeastern Arizona. Ever the wanderer, Hyman took charge in Harshaw, but his luck was no better there than it had been in Phoenix. One day—CRASH! An adobe wall collapsed, burying merchandise and leaving the store exposed to the elements. A flood later did more substantial damage, and finally, a fire in 1881 destroyed most of the store's remaining stock. Hyman once again found himself back in Phoenix, where he operated a variety store. A fire destroyed the block in which Hyman was located in May 1885, but the sixty-eight-year-old merchant promptly took off for San Francisco to buy goods for a new store. Eventually, Aaron, along with his younger brother David, backed this new venture. The old pioneer remained in Phoenix until his death in 1889. Aaron and David continued on in business as Goldberg Brothers well into the twentieth century.

Just as the experience of Hyman Goldberg demonstrated some of the hazards of doing business in territorial Arizona, as well as the resilience of its merchants, so did that of the Asher brothers and Guss Ellis. In 1878, Morris Asher of the defunct firm of Asher & Wollenburg moved from Prescott. He opened a similar operation on Washington Street. Morris left the firm shortly after the store's opening and was replaced by his brother Henry and Guss Ellis, brother of Hyman Ellis of Prescott. Asher & Ellis, however, also faltered and dissolved within a few months, its principals leaving town for a while.

Emil Ganz, from Tailor to Mayor

Phoenix boomed in the early 1880s. One of the town's leading attractions was a hotel, owned by a Jew, Emil Ganz. Born in the German duchy of Saxe-Meiningen, Ganz immigrated to New York in 1858, where he worked as a tailor before moving on to Philadelphia and, eventually, Georgia. He served in the Confederate army during the Civil War, winding up as a prisoner. At the conclusion of the war, he took a loyalty oath and received a train ticket home, but Georgia was barely recognizable. It was time to move west.

Ganz became a naturalized American citizen in 1866 and relocated to Kansas City and from there to Las Animas, Colorado. He worked as a tailor in both places. After marrying, he came to Prescott in 1874 with a load of merchandise, which he found he could not sell. He decided to open a saloon, but it, too, was not a success. He later recalled, "Business was not rushing." Ganz saw Prescott as nice, just not a place to make one's fortune.

In 1878–79, Ganz, having divorced his wife, decided to pull up stakes and move to Phoenix. There he converted a two-story brick office building into the Bank Exchange Hotel. Local newspapers boasted that the rooms were "well ventilated and handsomely furnished in suits [*sic*] and singles" and a balcony ran the length of the façade. The Bank Exchange also featured a bathhouse, reading and card rooms, a bar and a restaurant, complete with a French chef and "gentlemen of color" as waiters. The hotel became the growing town's social center, and Ganz and Bertha Angleman, a woman whom his Kansas City cousins picked out for him, married in 1883. They were among the elite of Phoenix society. Then, on April 26, 1885, the Bank Exchange burned to the ground along with thirteen other buildings. Ganz chose not to rebuild his hotel but stayed in Phoenix as a wholesale

Right: Studio portrait of Emil Ganz during his tenure as president of the National Bank of Arizona. *Courtesy Arizona Jewish Historical Society, Phoenix, Arizona.*

Below: Emil Ganz's Bank Exchange Hotel, Phoenix's leading hostelry until its destruction by fire. *Courtesy Arizona State Library, Archives and Public Records, History and Archives Division, #97-2129, Phoenix.*

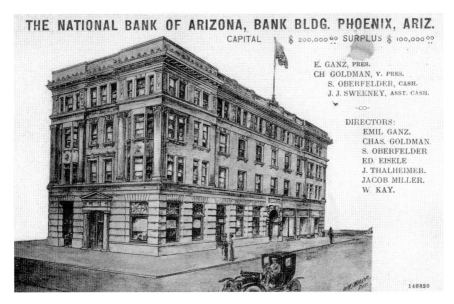

Early twentieth century advertising card showing the National Bank of Arizona building in Phoenix. *Courtesy Arizona Jewish Historical Society, Phoenix, Arizona.*

liquor merchant. He also entered the insurance and banking businesses and became president of the National Bank of Arizona in 1895.

In addition to his business interests, Ganz dabbled in city politics. A Democrat, he was elected mayor of Phoenix in 1885. He sought to make improvements to the streets and sidewalks, and his unfortunate experience with the Bank Exchange Hotel likely prompted a push for the establishment of a municipal fire department and waterworks. The city council initially refused his request, but a second major fire in August 1886 led voters to pass a bond issue to improve the town's water system and purchase firefighting equipment. More disagreements with the council, however, led to Ganz's resignation in late 1886. Although the council petitioned him to reconsider, he remained firm, stating that in return for his efforts he had received only "abuse and accusations." He moved to the West Coast, but soon was back in Arizona, serving as a director of the Arizona Territorial Insane Asylum. Ganz jumped back into politics with his election to the council in 1896 and as mayor three years later. This time, his Republican opponent was so weak that he did not even campaign. Soon after taking office, Ganz led a drive to annex residential neighborhoods contiguous to the city, and as a result, Phoenix grew considerably in area and population.

Ganz served two consecutive terms but lost his bid for another in May 1903. When he stepped down, the local press reflected that he had come to possess "a truly commendable knowledge of the affairs of his office, and a tactful way of adjusting differences and complications, which has won him the confidence and admiration of his fellow townsmen." Ganz remained president of the National Bank of Arizona until January 1920. Phoenix's pioneer hotelier and politician died in 1922.

A. Leonard Meyer, from Mayor to the Yuma Prison

In 1885, the year Emil Ganz won the mayoralty of Phoenix, another Jewish businessman also sought municipal office. Anton Leonard Meyer, a Russian Jew, had worked as a telegrapher and railway agent at a number of locations throughout the United States. By the early 1880s, he was living in Phoenix, where he ran the Wells Fargo office as well as agencies for several railway and steamship lines. He also owned his own express company, which hauled gold bullion from the mines of central Arizona to Phoenix for shipment by Wells Fargo to California. All of these activities made Meyer one of the most popular young businessmen in the Salt River valley. His popularity resulted in a victory in 1885 when he ran for Phoenix city treasurer as a Republican in a heavily Democratic town.

As treasurer, Meyer proved himself to be a careful administrator, and he easily won reelection. This race served as a prelude to May 1888, when Phoenix voters chose him as their mayor. His principal achievement came in January of the following year when the legislature selected the city to be the territorial capital. That spring, Meyer's term expired, and he did not choose to run for reelection. Instead, he ran for his old job as city treasurer, perhaps believing that this post offered better opportunities to enhance his own business interests. In the election, however, he was soundly defeated by Maurice Fleishman, manager of the Goldmans' liquor department.

The loss ended Meyer's political career, and he returned to Wells Fargo. But all was not well with Wells. Meyer began encountering difficulties in his dealings with the firm and suddenly disappeared in late 1889 under suspicious circumstances. Wells Fargo charged him with embezzling some $6,900 and offered a reward for his capture. Meyer, who had gone on the lam, finally surrendered in Victoria, British Columbia, and was returned to Arizona. Despite an able defense and a battery of character witnesses, he was found guilty and sentenced to five years in the Yuma Territorial Prison. In January 1891, however, Governor Nathan Oakes Murphy pardoned Meyer after being presented with a petition on his behalf signed by the territory attorney general, the prosecutor at his trial, a majority of the jurors and many Phoenix professionals and businessmen. After leaving prison, Meyer took his family to Mexico, where he worked as a railway agent, publicist and newspaper editor until his death in 1895 at the age of forty-four.

STOREKEEPING HAS ITS UPS AND DOWNS

Amid a flurry of optimism in the late 1870s and 1880s, Morris Asher returned to Phoenix and with Henry opened another short-lived dry goods house under the name M. Asher & Bro. Guss Ellis, too, sought to cash in on the apparent good times. He borrowed heavily to obtain a stock of merchandise and opened his own general store near M. Asher. Known as Guss Ellis & Co., the business concentrated on the agricultural trade. It seemed as though the new firm was off to a good start. Also marking a commercial milestone was the arrival from Prescott of Sol Lewis, who, with Martin Kales, opened a branch of the Bank of Arizona.

Advertising for Morris Asher's store offered Phoenicians just about anything they might need. *From* History of Arizona Territory, *1884.*

This prosperity, however, turned out to be an illusion. In an attempt to attract customers, Ellis was too liberal in extending credit, particularly to farmers and ranchers. In return for seed and supplies, he accepted liens on their land. When crops failed or grain or beef prices fell, as they did periodically, Guss then took possession of their property. This worked to his disadvantage, however, since often these holdings could not be easily or quickly resold, and Ellis's creditors wanted cash, not land in some distant desert valley. As a result, early in 1886, creditors, including Hyman Ellis, repossessed the assets of Guss Ellis & Co. and closed its doors. Although newspapers downplayed the seriousness of the crisis and loudly proclaimed Guss's honesty and integrity, it would be over a year before he again appeared on the Phoenix business scene.

Phoenix dry goods
merchant Morris Asher.
*Courtesy Sharlot Hall
Museum Library and Archives,
Prescott, Arizona.*

Guss returned to the dry goods business in Phoenix in September 1887. He partnered with his brother and former creditor Hyman in a large firm known as the Great Eastern Store. This time, however, more conservative business practices prevailed. Guss Ellis did well and later expanded his interests to include real estate and securities.

Not all merchants in Phoenix succumbed to the temptation of easy credit that trapped Guss Ellis. Nathan Rosenthal came from Fresno, California, in 1879 and opened a tobacco shop. Finding the market for such goods too limited, he arranged the purchase of the stock of a failed general store, bringing in L. Kutner of San Francisco as a partner and buyer. The firm prospered throughout the 1880s. Also entering the general merchandise business at this time was Marcus Jacobs, a Jewish immigrant from Prussia. Arriving in Phoenix in the late 1870s, he first found employment as a bookkeeper. Not content with this occupation, early the following decade, he joined with another Jewish merchant, Herbert Goodman, in the formation of an outlet for dry goods, groceries and provisions that remained in business through the turn of the century.

By the end of the 1880s, the population of Phoenix numbered over 3,100. Business remained generally good, and the Jewish community had become firmly established. Jews were proprietors of three of the town's five large general merchandise houses. Their influence extended throughout the Salt River valley and beyond to the mining and ranching districts and military posts of central Arizona, taking much of this trade away from Prescott. Believing in the economic future of the Salt River valley, Sol Lewis and Martin Kales disposed of their interest in Prescott's Bank of Arizona and obtained a federal charter for a new National Bank of Arizona in Phoenix in 1887. Among its backers were another Lewis brother, Meyer, and Charles Goldman. Sol Lewis's brother-in-law, banker Simon Oberfelder, came to Arizona and took care of the day-to-day operations. A few years later, hotelier turned securities dealer Emil Ganz became president of the National Bank, which remained a Phoenix institution until the mid-twentieth century.

The optimism of Sol Lewis and the others seemed confirmed in 1889, with the relocation of the territorial capital to Phoenix. During the early 1890s, however, the upswing began to level off. Flooding on the Salt River in 1890–91 caused a short-term business dislocation. The depression of 1893 was further complicated in Arizona by a severe drought. A number of stores went out of business, while the growth of most others slowed dramatically.

Department Stores and Specialty Shops

With the slow recovery of the valley's economy, new businesses opened. Three of these developed into large department stores in the twentieth century. Unlike the older general merchandise houses from which they evolved, the department stores were elaborate operations with considerable outlays for facilities, inventories and payroll. Stock was displayed in discrete departments, with considerably less clutter than in the old dry goods stores. They also did not continue the practice of selling everything from pincushions to plows. Department stores concentrated on clothing, furnishing goods, toys, housewares and, occasionally, furniture—merchandise desired by a growing, sophisticated urban middle class. The largest of the early Phoenix department stores was the New York Store, started by a young Jew from Russian Poland, Sam Korrick. Seeking to avoid conscription into the czar's army, he had come to the United States at age eighteen. With a slight build and dark hair, eyes and moustache, Sam had a ready smile and pleasing manner. He worked in El Paso for Isaac and Nathan Diamond as a clerk in their New

York Store. Moving to Phoenix, Sam established his own New York Store in 1895, located at first in a single twenty-five-by-forty-foot storefront on East Washington Street below the local Salvation Army headquarters. His initial shipment of merchandise arrived by train in September. Sam carted it by hand from the depot to his store, where he displayed it on packing crates. The store's entrance featured a large banner proclaiming the New York Store to be "The Cheapest Place in the City for Dry Goods, Clothing, Mens Furnishings, Notions, Boots & Shoes." When the counters finally arrived, they were covered in merchandise and the stock spilled out onto the sidewalk, but Sam assured customers that there would be "No Trouble to Show Goods." The store met with success, but perhaps Sam worked a bit too hard. He died unexpectedly at thirty-three in 1903. The business passed to his younger brother Charles. Still a minor, Charles received guidance from his guardian, banker Simon Oberfelder. Aided financially and personally by Oberfelder, Charles conducted a prosperous business until he came of age four years later. In 1906, Charles asked his younger brother Abe to join him as the store's merchandise manager.

By 1909, the New York Store had expanded to encompass several storefronts along East Washington with separate departments for dry goods, clothing, hats and so on. As the territorial period ended, the

Russian immigrant Sam Korrick (*center in dark suit and derby*) established the New York Store in Phoenix. His brothers Charles and Abe developed it into a major department store. *Courtesy Arizona Jewish Historical Society, Phoenix, Arizona.*

Charles Korrick in front of the New York Store about 1903. *Author's collection.*

Korrick brothers realized that the firm had outgrown these facilities and would need a new building. The result would be a multilevel structure with a cooling system and elevator, located at the corner of First Street and Washington. Merchandise would be arrayed in counters and in polished wood and glass cabinets. When it opened in November 1914, Korrick's, as it came to be known, was the city's leading downtown department store, catering to the fashion and household needs of Phoenix women and men.

Not long after Sam Korrick arrived in Phoenix, another major dry goods company with a familiar name came to town. Unlike Morris Goldwater, his brother Baron had ambitions for the family business

Korrick's department store sold merchandise in a large, airy building. This was quite a change from the narrow, crowded general stores of the nineteenth century. *Author's collection.*

beyond the comfortable confines of Prescott. He saw the Salt River valley as the coming region of Arizona and felt J. Goldwater & Bros. needed to be a part of it. Morris, who remembered well the unsuccessful venture of the 1870s, had his doubts. The Prescott store was running just fine and making a tidy income. But Baron was not to be denied. According to Goldwater family legend, in 1894 he challenged Morris to a hand of the card game casino to settle the issue. Morris lost and agreed to join with Baron and brother Henry in the opening of a Phoenix store. The elder Goldwater, however, insisted that the company's headquarters remain in Prescott. Phoenix would be just a branch. Baron and Morris worked feverishly to get the store ready for its March 21, 1896 debut. When it opened, the Goldwater emporium featured not only new and elegant counters and shelves but also electric lighting and a telephone. Unlike previous Goldwater endeavors that had relied on goods from San Francisco, the Phoenix store specialized in merchandise ordered directly from eastern markets and manufacturers. Stock would be of the highest quality, not, "the meaner sorts of merchandise." Baron ran the operation, causing Henry to gradually lose interest and leave the firm.

Handsome, impeccably dressed and outgoing, Baron was a natural salesman, and he imbued his staff with the same enthusiasm. Thanks largely to his leadership, the store proved to be a success and within a couple of years outgrew its original quarters. He rented a larger location on North First Street between Washington and Adams, transferring the best merchandise, and on January 3, 1899, the new store launched amid music and entertainment. It, too, enjoyed immediate success. Goldwater's became known for purveying the finest and most up-to-date ladies' fashions. Lest the men felt left out, Baron also opened an annex farther down East Washington to serve as an outlet for ready-to-wear suits and coats. As the twentieth century dawned, despite Morris's initial misgivings, Baron had made Phoenix for all practical purposes the center for the Goldwater family's commercial enterprises.

The third department store to open in Phoenix came about through the efforts of two Polish Jews, Nathan Diamond and his brother, Isaac. The Diamond brothers came to the United States in 1888 via England and eventually found their way out west. Since 1891, they had been operating the New York Store, a dry goods outlet, in El Paso. The store was doing satisfactorily, but in 1897 the brothers decided to give the Salt River valley a try. They probably learned about the potential of the Phoenix area from their former employee Sam Korrick. Since Sam had already taken the New York Store name, the Diamonds called their branch the Boston Store. Located a few steps down the street from Korrick's, the new venture proved so successful that by 1900 the Diamonds had closed out in El Paso and transferred their business to Phoenix. The Boston Store quickly outgrew its initial East Washington quarters and moved to a larger two-story building on the same street. With the extra space, the Diamond brothers were able to reorganize to feature individual merchandise departments—clothing, dry goods, hats, shoes and furnishings—making theirs a true department store. A devastating fire in 1907 almost put the Boston Store out of business, but the Diamonds had inventory in an off-site warehouse and were able to weather this disaster. A six-month-long fire sale followed, and soon the Boston Store was back offering competition to the Korricks and Goldwaters.

While the opening of the Korrick, Goldwater and Diamond department stores testified to Phoenix's commercial maturity, most Jews during the later territorial period either clerked for the larger firms or operated specialty businesses. The Goldmans became wholesale grocers and dealers in agricultural implements. Herbert Goodman opened a

Right: Baron Goldwater, founder of the Phoenix Goldwater's department store, with his son Barry. *Courtesy Arizona Jewish Historical Society, Phoenix, Arizona.*

Below: Isaac and Nathan Diamond established Phoenix's Boston Store, later Diamond's department store. They must have had financial difficulties at this time. Goldwater's annex is next door. *Courtesy Arizona Jewish Historical Society, Phoenix, Arizona.*

Since 1897, the Rosenzweig store in downtown Phoenix has offered a variety of rings, bracelets, watches, necklaces, broches and other fine jewelry. *Courtesy Arizona Jewish Historical Society, Phoenix, Arizona.*

pharmacy. And in the late 1880s, the Goldberg brothers shifted from general merchandise to men's clothing. During this time, Aaron Goldberg devoted much of his time to civic and political matters. He served in the Nineteenth Territorial Legislature, where, in 1897, he introduced the bill authorizing $100,000 in bonds for the construction of the territorial capitol in Phoenix.

By the coming of statehood in 1912, over half of the tailors and clothiers in Phoenix were Jews. One of the most notable, some would say notorious, was tailor Henry Rosenstein, who also occasionally went by the alias of Henry Rubenstein. His antics with the local demimonde, including running his own bordello, earned him the stern disapproval of proper Phoenicians. Nevertheless, he was a success at his legitimate trade and remained in business selling tailored suits for many years. Less colorful, but equally successful, were Adolph and Nathan Herzberg and Leonard and Sydney Wolf, the latter stating they would sell men's suits for $12.50 from their store, "Right in town, but away from the high rent district."

Tobacconists Selim Michaelson, Sam Seip and brothers Harry and Louis Baswitz also were familiar members of the business community, as were jewelers Nathan Friedman and Isaac Rosensweig. Liquor dealers and brothers William, Joseph and Louis Melczer expanded from San Francisco and Los Angeles, where the family had prosperous liquor businesses. Locating first in Nogales, Louis moved to Phoenix in 1893. The firm purchased the liquor department of Goldman & Company and then Emil Ganz's wholesale liquor distributorship, making Melczer Brothers the largest such firm in the territory during the early twentieth century. By the end of the territorial period, Phoenix was, indeed, the commercial hub of Arizona.

4

WHEN THE OLD PUEBLO
WAS YOUNG

Phoenix may have been Arizona's political and economic center and an urban oasis by the late territorial period, but for much of the middle and late nineteenth century, Tucson reigned as the metropolis. Not until the decade between 1910 and 1920 did Phoenix surpass Tucson in population. Located along major wagon, stagecoach and, later, railroad routes, Tucson was for a while the territory's capital and center for commerce. Referred to as the Old Pueblo, Tucson's large-scale merchandise houses dominated business in southern and eastern Arizona, with their influence being felt as far north as the Salt River valley.

"Everything that Has Some Money in It"

It was hot the day in 1867 when Lionel and Barron Jacobs arrived in Tucson. The calendar said fall, but the heat persisted. The two young brothers had just driven a wagon full of canned goods and a small assortment of general merchandise all the way from San Bernardino, California. They were determined to make themselves merchant princes.

Lionel and younger brother Barron were the sons of Mark Israel Jacobs. He was born in Poland in 1816 and twelve years later moved with his father to Manchester, England, where he learned the clothing business, married Hannah Solomon and started a family. They all immigrated to Baltimore in the early 1840s, but the lure of the Gold Rush prompted a move to California

Tucson merchant and banker Lionel Jacobs. *Courtesy Arizona Historical Society, #1804, Tucson, Arizona.*

Barron Jacobs, brother of Lionel and partner in their many enterprises. *Courtesy Arizona Historical Society, #3924, Tucson, Arizona.*

in 1851. Two of twelve siblings, Lionel, born in England, and Barron, born in Baltimore, grew up in San Diego, where Mark operated a general store and news depot. In 1857, the family moved again, this time to San Bernardino, where their sister Leah lived. San Diego was a pleasant town but a bit sleepy and out of the way, while San Bernardino was booming. Due to San Bernardino's location on the main road from the east, Overland Mail stagecoaches stopped there, as did travelers heading to and from the gold fields. Lionel went to work for Mark Jacobs and Company in 1861, followed by Barron the following year. Like Mike and Joe Goldwater, Lionel and Barron Jacobs differed in both appearance and personality. Tall and debonair, Lionel was an outdoorsman, outgoing and sociable. Barron was short, stocky, quiet and more bookish. But the brothers had a strong bond that they would need in Arizona.

In the spring of 1867, Mark Jacobs learned that the territorial capital and military headquarters in Arizona would soon relocate from Prescott to Tucson. The town was bound to prosper, so he sent Lionel and Barron across the mountains and deserts of Southern California to Arizona. The trip took over two months, and by the time they reached Tucson, the brothers had long since shed the dress suits they had worn on their departure. Daytime temperatures rose to well over one hundred degrees as they pushed through stands of saguaro, prickly pear and cholla cacti. The brothers shivered at night as they slept in the wagon to avoid rattlesnakes, scorpions and tarantulas. They also kept a keen eye out for Indians who were known to ambush lone travelers. Arriving just outside of Tucson, they made camp, and Barron scouted out a suitable location for the store. What met his eyes was a far cry from the prosperous settlement Mark had envisioned.

None of the streets were paved, and dust clouds swirled as wagons, cavalry troops and occasional livestock herds plodded down them. Winter rains and summer thunderstorms turned streets to bogs and compelled owners of the many adobe buildings to make constant repairs. Having no permanent residence, the territorial legislature occasionally met in Charles Brown's Congress Hall Saloon. Nevertheless, Tucson was clearly the metropolis of the Arizona Territory, with a population in the neighborhood of two thousand.

Lionel and Barron encountered other Jews in Tucson—Nathan Appel, Frenchy Lazard, Philip Drachman, Alexander Levin and William Zeckendorf. But the brothers found that their main competition would come from the town's largest store, Lord & Williams. Hoping to attract some of Lord & Williams's customers, Lionel and Barron rented a dirt floored adobe next door. Heeding their father's instruction to "do everything that has some money in it," they unloaded the wagon, hammered together some shelves and counters, cleaned up, donned fresh clothes and threw open the entrance to M.I. Jacobs & Company. Within a week, they had sold all of their stock.

Giddy with their initial success, the brothers looked to become permanent fixtures in Tucson. They sold their wagon and mules and used some of the proceeds to make improvements to the store, including a wood floor and a new counter and shelves. The remaining funds, along with profits from the sale, went to buy more merchandise. They had only two weeks to wait because Mark already had borrowed on his San Bernardino store to pay for more goods. This shipment also sold out quickly. Within three months, a second shipment had arrived, followed by a third, and Tucsonans were starting to pay attention to these two new entrepreneurs.

When the fourth consignment ended up on the bottom of the Colorado River due to an accident, however, things turned sour. Mark had obtained the goods on credit and counted on the transfer of funds from Tucson to pay his creditors. When this failed to come through, he went bankrupt and closed the San Bernardino store. M.I. Jacobs & Co. in Tucson also was forced to close after not quite a year in business, but rather than returning to California, Lionel and Barron took odd jobs and remained in Tucson.

Once Mark had settled his debts, he moved to San Francisco. There he scraped together enough money to pay cash for another load for Arizona. The brothers streamlined the transportation arrangements, paying a bit extra to hire respected forwarding agent David Neahr of Yuma to see that goods arrived safely and on time. The shipment did indeed arrive with no problems, and the brothers greeted it with delight. Lionel and Barron Jacobs were in Tucson to stay.

Shipping bills reflected the nature of the business. On January 12, 1870, Neahr forwarded to the Jacobs brothers in Tucson:

35 cases of books and shoes
6 trunks of general merchandise
2 cases of general merchandise
1 pair of watches
1 case of powder
1 case of salmon

Later that year, the steamer *Orizaba* reported the following consignment for M.I. Jacobs & Company:

Pants—including fancy satin pants
Shawls
Saddles
Sheeting
Shirts
Bridles
Under and over shirts
Shoes
Cigar papers
Coverlids

At the time, the brothers also seemed to be dealing in pharmaceuticals, or at least supplying a local druggist, since on April 22, 1870, C.F. Richards of San Francisco sent them an order of:

Sarsaparilla
Epsom salts
Sassafras bark
Prescription vials and corks

Ginger
Camphor
Ground flax seed
Eye water
Syringes

Within five years, the firm had expanded to include home furnishings for Tucson's growing middle class, as a shipping bill from the steamer *Montana* indicated:

To David Neahr for L. M. Jacobs & Co.—
3 cases furniture
2 cases furniture, knockdown
1 case marble
1 case looking glasses
1 case glassware

Besides purchasing merchandise for the Tucson store, Mark Jacobs kept a close eye on the San Francisco money market. Through weekly letters, he informed his sons about current exchange rates for gold, Mexican silver dollars and U.S. greenbacks. This was vital information, since the Arizona Territory was plagued by a lack of hard currency and the reluctance of financial houses to extend credit to frontier merchants at favorable rates. In Tucson, many transactions involved Mexican silver currency, the so-called 'dobe dollars. Some customers paid with checks or drafts on California or eastern banks, and contractors providing goods or services to the military received vouchers, both of which could take a long time to redeem. Soldiers also received their pay in paper greenbacks, and merchants discounted these. The information Mark provided about the value of silver dollars, drafts, vouchers and greenbacks in relation to American gold coinage (which creditors required for the payment of debts) enabled the brothers to calculate the most advantageous prices to charge for goods. Knowledge of currency rates also aided in a lucrative monetary exchange business. Mark would send gold from San Francisco to Tucson, where greenbacks were rather plentiful but specie was rare. Lionel and Barron then converted the gold at a favorable rate into paper money, which they sent to San Francisco for sale at a profit.

The Brothers Strike Out on Their Own

The business ties between the Jacobs brothers and their father had resulted in a successful commercial enterprise, but personal differences were another matter. Mark's daughter Julia died in 1871, followed by Hannah the following year. These tragedies sent the elder Jacobs into a downward spiral for months, during which time he lost much of his interest in the family business. The embezzlement of money by another son, Albert, in San Francisco added to his troubles. Albert was banished to Tucson for a time as punishment, while in 1873 Lionel went to San Francisco to sort things out.

But the situation did not improve. Mark's infatuation with and marriage proposal to a sixteen-year-old girl in 1874 provoked a family crisis. For his sons, particularly Lionel, this was the last straw. Mark had increasingly tried to control the entire operation from San Francisco, while Lionel and Barron, familiar with conditions in Arizona, believed they knew better. Mark's letters were full of unsolicited admonitions and maxims that irked the brothers no end. By the end of 1874, Lionel's relations with his father had deteriorated to the point that he was "really very anxious to close out" with Mark. Barron went along, and in March of the following year, M.I. Jacobs and Company dissolved. Lionel assumed control of a new firm, L.M. Jacobs and Company, with Barron and another Jewish associate, Leopold Wolf. Mark continued to advise the company on financial and commercial matters, mostly through letters to Barron, with whom he maintained a more cordial correspondence. Lionel and Wolf, however, took on the tasks of purchasing and forwarding goods, which caused them to spend more time in San Francisco and New York. Barron mostly stayed in Tucson to mind the store, keep the accounts and let Lionel and Wolf know what merchandise to buy. This arrangement worked, and few customers recognized any difference in the way the business operated.

By the time the Jacobs brothers decided to heed one of their father's suggestions to "deal less in calico and more in money" and establish the Pima County Bank in 1879, they had become fixtures both in Tucson's commercial world and social scene. They had realized their dream of becoming the town's merchant princes and were regulars at the local saloons, where much business also was done. They gambled (though not to excess), bet on cockfights, rode and raced horses, hunted wild game, took part in sharpshooting matches and more than occasionally visited the dance halls and sporting houses of the town's "Wedge" block and "Maiden Lane."

Within a couple of decades of arriving in Tucson, Lionel and Barron Jacobs were proprietors of the Jacobs Block, not far from the infamous "Wedge." *Courtesy Arizona State Library, Archives and Public Records, History and Archives Division, #97-5656, Phoenix.*

Barron and Lionel closed the store in 1880 and had disposed of the last of their mercantile interests by 1883. Over the next three decades, they concentrated on banking and helped found the Arizona Banking Association in 1903. The brothers retired from business in 1913, appropriately enough just after the end of the territorial era. From purveyors of a wagonload of canned goods in 1867, they had become millionaires.

"Irrepressible Z"

Just before Lionel and Barron Jacobs first left California for Tucson, another Jewish family that would make its mark in the pueblo arrived, this one from the east. Brothers Aaron, Louis and William Zeckendorf hailed from the village of Hemmendorf in the Baden-Wurttemberg district of Germany. In 1853, Aaron joined his cousins, the successful Spiegelberg brothers, in Santa Fe, New Mexico. The Spiegelbergs had been involved in commerce in New Mexico since before the Mexican War. Aaron clerked in their mercantile establishment for a year, learning the trade and earning enough money (along with a loan from his cousins) to open his own general store in Santa Fe.

After immigrating to the United States, and spending some time as a pack peddler in New York, Louis made his way west and drove an ox team to Santa Fe, arriving in 1855. After reuniting with his brother Aaron, Louis moved on to Albuquerque, and Aaron and Louis formed A. and L. Zeckendorf. Their younger brother, William, also arrived in New Mexico in 1857 and began working for the family business, dividing his time between the two stores. When the Confederates invaded the territory in 1862, William enlisted in the Union's First New Mexican Regiment. He became a lieutenant and, because of his mercantile experience, the unit's assistant quartermaster, participating in the battles at Valverde, Socorro and Glorieta Pass. In the meantime, A. and L. Zeckendorf suffered due to confiscation of goods and taxes imposed by the Confederates who had occupied Albuquerque and Santa Fe in March 1862. Even after the Rebels were driven south, businesses still had to deal with a lack of currency and merchandise. The Zeckendorfs once again had to rely on the more established Spiegelbergs to keep their stores afloat. They also supplemented their income by obtaining a mail contract.

The mail business brought the Zeckendorfs to Arizona in 1866. With Sol Barth, they obtained a government contract to transport mail between Prescott and Tubac. The partnership dissolved later that year, and Aaron took over the route. Although he hired a driver to carry the mail, he traveled about the territory making sure that the business operated smoothly. While visiting Tucson, the elder Zeckendorf saw an opportunity to make some money. The few shops in the pueblo carried a limited supply of merchandise. In the fall of 1866, therefore, he loaded up several wagonloads of excess goods from the Albuquerque store and set out for Tucson.

After weeks on the trail, the reception Aaron received must have both surprised and delighted him. Established storekeepers, happy to be able to obtain new merchandise and perhaps looking to squelch some competition, quickly bought up almost all of his goods. His success only encouraged the Zeckendorf brothers to expand their business. Before long, they had rented a building and opened a branch of A. and L. Zeckendorf on Pearl Street with Philip Drachman as manager. Philip's son Harry recalled that his father had to make regular trips to Los Angeles to deposit the store's receipts, as there was no safe place in the pueblo to store large sums of money.

The success of the Tucson store, along with the relocation of the territorial capital from Prescott in 1867 and a general upswing in Arizona's economy, prompted the Zeckendorfs to make the operation there permanent the following year. William became manager of the branch, and Drachman left for a visit to New York. There he became a part of the extended Zeckendorf

For a number of years, the Zeckendorf's adobe store in Tucson seemed in constant need of repairs. *Courtesy Arizona Historical Society, #5679, Tucson, Arizona.*

family by marrying one of the cousins, Rosa Katzenstein. Louis Zeckendorf also went to New York, but for a different reason. He wanted to make his home there and see to the purchasing and forwarding of merchandise to the firm's southwestern outlets. Aaron returned to Albuquerque to manage the New Mexico stores.

Stock for the Zeckendorf store traveled from the East by rail to the warehouses of freighters in Kansas and Colorado. Wagon trains then hauled the goods to New Mexico over the Santa Fe Trail. William would regularly journey to Albuquerque to meet the trains and arrange for transportation of the Arizona merchandise. Bulky freight wagons, laden with tons of items ranging from diamond stickpins to crowbars, with William in the lead, became a common sight pulling up on the street in front of the Zeckendorf establishment at the corner of Main and Pennington streets.

While Aaron and Louis prospered in the Southwest, they never adopted a frontier mentality or lifestyle. The same could not be said of William. His free spirit manifested itself in Tucson. The fact that he wore spectacles belied his true nature. Far from the constraints of his staid brothers and accepted norms of the "civilized" East, he assumed the persona of a frontiersman. He drank and gambled (sometimes to excess) and joined with the Jacobs brothers and the town's other businessmen in expeditions to the "Wedge" and "Maiden Lane." William learned how to handle a gun and used his six-shooter to foil burglars breaking into the store. He chased down Apache cattle thieves and took at least one scalp, which he kept as a souvenir. His activities soon made him somewhat of a local celebrity. Particularly fond of fireworks, he treated Tucsonans to pyrotechnic displays on almost every occasion. At one such event, an errant rocket started a fire that threatened the town. He also became the principal organizer and overseer of parades, *bailes* (dances) and fiestas, including the annual weeklong blowout called Fiesta de San Augustin. He even portrayed Santa Claus for the pueblo's children at Christmastime. Little wonder the local press referred to him as the "Irrepressible Z!"

While William's antics earned the disapproval of his brothers, they would probably have ignored his exploits had the store continued making money. Indeed, its initial success had prompted them to begin closing out their Albuquerque store to concentrate on southern Arizona. Unfortunately, while throwing parties and hanging out with the "boys" in saloons, William increasingly neglected his most important responsibility—the business. By 1870, it was one of the largest mercantile concerns in Tucson, with a big store and warehouse and stock worth over $100,000. To help manage the operation, and probably free up his time for more pleasurable activities, William hired a Hungarian Jew named Theodore Welisch and his wife, Julia. They arrived in Tucson in 1871 and went right to work for Zeckendorf, although their lack of knowledge of English and Spanish put them at a disadvantage. William seemed not to care, just so long as there was someone other than himself behind the counter.

That year, Aaron paid a visit to Tucson to check on the store. Although the business still turned a profit, William did not seem to pay much attention to it. Aaron gave his brother a talking-to about his responsibilities and then returned to Albuquerque to continue planning the move to Arizona. He must have had an inkling that William might not heed his advice, however, since on a trip to New York, he mentioned to Louis that, given the size of the Tucson store and its merchandise, income was a bit on the low side. This raised a red flag. Louis made an inspection visit in 1872, and what he found appalled the no-nonsense merchant. He wrote Aaron that William's "deportment" was that of "a man without the slightest virtue, but possessed of all imaginable vices." Even worse, he did not even make a pretense of minding the store. On those rare occasions when he did find himself behind the counter, William catered to the "commonest trade," mostly Mexicans, and neglected to stock more profitable fancy goods. Despite the earnest efforts of Theodore and Julia, whom Louis felt had been kept in virtual slavery, sales were low and continuing to fall.

While William made himself scarce, Louis sought to rectify things. He cleaned and painted the store, brought order to the disorganized merchandise counters and sought to drum up business among the pueblo's Anglo population. Then he and Theodore conducted a thorough inventory. They found much of the stock dirty and damaged. They even opened boxes of shoes and boots only to find many of them mismatched. There were duplicate orders and orders that had never been filled. William had to go.

Indeed, William probably would have been sacked right then had not Aaron died suddenly in February 1872. With his brother still indifferent about the business, it was up to Louis to figure out what to do. He sent for his seventeen-year-old nephew, Albert Steinfeld, who had been living in Denver, to come and assist with the store. Albert traveled by train to San Francisco, then by steamer to San Diego and finally a six-day stagecoach ride to Tucson. After such an arduous journey, he found his destination to be hardly worth the effort, later recalling:

> *I did not expect much, but even in this respect I was disappointed, and wondered if I had made a mistake in coming. I was very tired, worn out by the long stage trip....I went to bed early and cried myself to sleep.*

But Albert had made an agreement, and that was his bond. Once in Tucson, he joined Louis and Theodore in getting the business ready for sale because the elder Zeckendorf had concluded that without Aaron, the store could not succeed. During this period, they continued selling merchandise, and oddly enough, receipts picked up. Since a ready buyer could not be found anyway, Louis changed his mind and decided to keep going. William would remain nominally in charge, with the real work being done by the employees. Louis returned to New York, but when William still declined to take an active role, he decided that Steinfeld and Welisch did not have quite the experience to run such a large concern. Reluctantly, therefore, he trudged back to the pueblo, arriving in February 1873. He dissolved the old partnership, now moot because of Aaron's death, and announced that the business would be known as Louis Zeckendorf. Louis, however, missed New York. He was not the frontiersman his brother was. After a few months, he arranged for the sale of the store's stock and accounts to Albert and Theodore, who demonstrated that they could handle the job. Wisely, Louis kept ownership of the building and its fixtures.

Louis left for San Francisco and New York soon after the sale. Although the new firm changed its name to Zeckendorf and Welisch, Albert and Theodore did all of the work. William continued his Wild West ways, absenting himself from the store as often as he could. The arrangement could not last. Theodore became annoyed with his partner's neglect of the business, and after considerable legal wrangling, Zeckendorf and Welisch dissolved on November 21, 1873.

Theodore Welisch landed on his feet and went on to establish his own store. After the breakup, William, however, had little ready cash, most of his assets being tied up in inventory. This situation left Louis in a quandary. William still owed him a considerable sum from his original sale of the business, and if he left his brother to flounder, he would not see a dime. As much as he distrusted William's business sense, therefore, Louis again had to go to Tucson and make an arrangement with his brother. The result was a new venture, Zeckendorf Brothers, located in the Main and Pennington building, with William nominally in charge.

Louis headed back to New York. He reasoned correctly that Albert Steinfeld and a clerk named Westmeyer who had come from the firm's store in Rio Mimbres, New Mexico, would ensure the prosperity of Zeckendorf Brothers. William, meanwhile, continued to self-promote and dabble in mining by grubstaking prospectors. Then, in March 1875, he left for New York, supposedly on a business trip. When he returned, he was a changed and married man. Louis, believing that having a family would prompt his brother to focus more on the business, had arranged for William to meet Julia Frank, daughter of a clothing merchant. They were wed on October 25, leaving for Tucson soon thereafter. When William returned to the pueblo, however, things were not quite the same. While still affable and civic-minded, he no longer was the Irrepressible Z, interested only in gambling and fiestas. He was now thirty-three; perhaps he had matured a bit. So, with a wife, whom he adored, and later a daughter, Hilda, to support, William at last turned his energies to the store.

ZECKENDORF BROTHERS

With William now more attentive to the business, the Zeckendorfs prospered. The brothers themselves, however, still could not get along. Their personalities differed too much. They squabbled off and on until 1878, when William finally left the partnership. He and Julia announced that they would soon depart on a trip to Europe and intended to relocate permanently to New York. Their departure was not soon enough for Louis, who hurried back to Tucson to reorganize the store again. This time he wisely took in Albert Steinfeld as managing partner, although the store would operate under the name L. Zeckendorf and Company.

In Steinfeld, Louis had found the perfect manager. He was meticulous, knowledgeable about wholesale and retail merchandising and determined to succeed. Louis could return to New York to oversee the firm's purchasing, contracting and credit operations and not worry about emergency trips to the Southwest. For his part, Albert began making improvements to the store. He did his best to keep the crumbling adobe neat and clean, with merchandise attractively displayed. To assist him, he hired a friend from his childhood days in Germany, Leo Goldschmidt, whose sister happened to be Aaron Zeckendorf's widow. Leo had been working for the Spiegelbergs in New Mexico and was glad to move to Tucson. He and Steinfeld became great companions, working and sharing a house together. When, after a short time in the employ of Zeckendorf, Leo decided to go out on his own, Albert loaned him the money to open a furniture store.

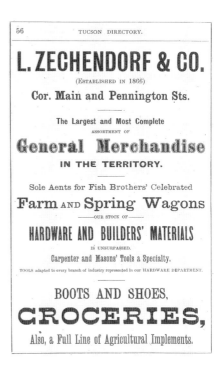

While the printer of the 1881 Tucson directory may have misspelled the name, there could be no doubt that Zeckendorf's sold a wide variety of goods. *Author's collection.*

While Albert guided the growth of L. Zeckendorf and Company, competition appeared from a most unlikely source. William had not yet left Tucson when he was contacted by wealthy New Mexico merchant and distant cousin, Zadoc Staab, who wished to open a store with him in Tucson. Once the contract was signed, William leased space (next door to L. Zeckendorf!) and made other arrangements for opening the store. Wagonloads of general merchandise from New York soon clogged the street in front of the new store, and Zeckendorf and Staab opened for business in November 1878.

Although adjacent to L. Zeckendorf & Company, William let it be known widely that his store had nothing to do with it. In a thinly veiled reference to his brother's business, he stated: "As to competition in this market, five minutes will convince you who is Boss, Zeckendorf & Staab." One can only imagine the cold stares that must have passed between William and Albert Steinfeld as they unlocked their respective doors each morning.

Less than two years later, an event occurred that turned the Tucson commercial community on its ear. Trains of the Southern Pacific Railroad steamed into town in March 1880. While just about everyone hailed the coming of the iron horse and anticipated eagerly the prosperity that would ensue, the initial result was a retrenchment in business. Heretofore, merchants had to maintain full warehouses so that their inventories would not be depleted during the often lengthy periods between the arrival of the wagons. Now fresh goods could be shipped directly from California or the East in a matter of days and at a fraction of the cost. The first regularly scheduled freight train to arrive in Tucson was loaded with new goods for L. Zeckendorf. The arrival of the railroad, however, did cause some distress, as in the case of L. Meyer and Company. The firm opened the California Store in Tucson in 1878. With its main office in San Francisco, the firm prospered by buying up stocks of bankrupt California companies and then shipping them to Arizona for resale. L. Meyer advertised these goods at prices "less than you can buy Eastern Trash" (a possible swipe at the Zeckendorfs). The reduced cost of importing by rail, however, meant that Meyer's prices were now no better, and in some cases higher, for goods of higher quality. The company found itself quickly driven into bankruptcy. A number of other stores followed suit. Instead of a boom, Tucson experienced a fire sale.

Fortunately, both Zeckendorfs were nimble enough to adjust and their stores survived. Soon after the arrival of the railroad, Albert Steinfeld started advocating for a larger, more modern building—brick with large attractive display windows. He finally got his way, and in April 1882, the new store opened. It was 85 by 188 feet, with a mostly glass front, and lighted by electricity from Tucson's first fledgling electric power company. With the local press calling it the "Greatest Store Between San Francisco and St. Louis," it seemed as though Tucson and L. Zeckendorf had, indeed, arrived.

While L. Zeckendorf set a new standard for commercial enterprises in Tucson, William was in trouble. Although he made it through the downturn that followed the arrival of the Southern Pacific, it was a tumultuous time. In early 1880, newspapers announced the dissolution of the firm of

Louis Zeckendorf's second Tucson store, a much larger and better constructed building than the old adobe. *From History of Arizona Territory Showing its Resources and Advantages with Illustrations, San Francisco: Wallace W. Elliott, 1884.*

Zeckendorf & Staab. What precipitated the breakup is unclear. It is possible that Staab wanted to expand and modernize while the more easygoing William wanted to keep things pretty much as they were. Staab might have followed through with this, having purchased some commercial lots in Tucson, but he died in 1884 before acting on his plan. For his part, William persevered, establishing himself as William Zeckendorf, "Dealer in General Merchandise." A fire caused by an exploding lamp the following August, however, destroyed the retail, clothing and hat departments. A disagreement with Southern Pacific over freight rates did not help matters. Finally, William's own practice of extending credit too liberally and too many bad accounts brought the business crashing down. Lionel Jacobs and the First National Bank assumed control of the assets of the firm.

Being declared an insolvent debtor in March 1885, William became a silent partner in the general merchandise house of J. Frank and Company. Backed by nephews Albert and Adolph Steinfeld, with whom he had come to an understanding, and with money from his wife's family, he reacquired his old Main Street store. He finally turned the business over to a manager and left Tucson for New York in July 1891. For a while, his name remained prominent in Tucson through the failure of J. Frank and Company in October and proceedings against him for payment of long-standing debts. William died in Far Rockaway, New York, in 1906. With his death passed the era of Tucson's colorful pioneer general merchants.

Louis Zeckendorf must have breathed a sigh of relief when his brother at last retired from business in 1891, but by the late nineteenth century, his own interest in the Arizona store had begun to wane. Profits were good and he still made occasional trips out west to keep in touch with conditions. Each visit, however, seemed more and more like an unwanted errand. Besides, under Steinfeld's able management, the firm had grown to include Leo Goldschmidt's former furniture store across Pennington, which now housed rugs, linoleum, furniture, drapes and wallpapers, and a large warehouse along the Southern Pacific tracks. Although L. Zeckendorf prospered under Steinfeld's leadership, around the turn of the twentieth century, the two men began quarreling over management style and some of the firm's mining properties. The partnership dissolved, and after 1904, Louis remained in New York, where he looked after other business interests and where he died in 1937 at the age of ninety-eight.

With the dissolution of the partnership, Steinfeld assumed full control

OUR MEN'S DEPARTMENT

Clothing for Men Who Know

"Fashion Clothes"

are for the upper tendom—the top notchers who know what's what and are proud of it.
Wear a suit of "Fashion Clothes" and the world will give you the glad hand and call you by your front name.
Because "Fashion Clothes" are not just clothes they are creations in fine fabrics and revatations in choice styles.
For young men, price $15 to $40.
Every suit guaranteed.

Albert Steinfeld & Co.

Less than three decades after Zeckendorf's notice appeared in the Tucson directory, advertising for the store's successor, Albert Steinfeld and Company, reflected the territory's new sophistication. *Author's collection.*

of L. Zeckendorf. Some Tucsonans worried that the firm would pull out of town completely, but Albert quickly scotched these rumors. He renamed the firm Albert Steinfeld & Company, and although he received a rent-free lease for a year on the store as part of the settlement, he soon began work on a new building at the corner of Stone and Pennington. The multilevel concrete and steel structure housed all of the business's retail and wholesale grocery, liquor and hardware departments and offices under one roof. It employed some 150 men and women, and at the grand opening on the evening of March 15, 1906, an orchestra played and the first 2,500 customers through the doors received souvenir silver bowls. Boosters called it the greatest department store between El Paso and Los Angeles, even San Francisco. For good reason, the local press hailed Steinfeld as "Arizona's Merchant Prince," snatching that title from the Jacobs brothers. He began turning more and more responsibility over to his son Harold in the 1920s. Nevertheless, Albert, who stated that he would rather "wear out than rust out," kept a hand in the business until his death on February 8, 1935. His legacy lived on, as Steinfeld's remained a major department store in southern Arizona into the mid-twentieth century.

NOT QUITE *TENDEJONES*

No, they were not *tendejones*—the Mexican term for a small shop owner, usually operating in a hut or shanty and selling cheap goods—but small businesses accounted for the livelihoods of most Jews who came to territorial Tucson. A few, like the Jacobs brothers and Zeckendorfs, started modestly and grew to be merchant princes, but they proved to be the exception rather than the rule. The Jacobs, Zeckendorf and Steinfeld stores presented the bright face of Tucson's economy during the territorial period, but Jewish-owned small businesses and specialty shops were its backbone.

The majority of Jewish storekeepers tended to their businesses to achieve a comfortable middle-class life. Their stores lined the adobe blocks that made up Tucson's commercial district. Most sold dry goods or clothing, but others dealt in liquor, beer and entertainment, tobacco, groceries, jewelry and other lines. Some did well. Many did not. Those who succeeded, however, made a decent living and comprised the town's growing middle class.

Beginning in the late 1860s, the firm of H. Lesinsky and Company maintained a modest dry goods outlet. German Jew Henry Lesinsky had prospected for gold unsuccessfully in Australia and California. He was a nephew of prominent Las Cruces businessman Julius Freudenthal, who maintained stores throughout southern New Mexico. Henry went to work for his uncle in the late 1850s, and the Tucson store may have been the western branch of this larger firm, which came to be known as Lesinsky and Freudenthal. Henry's brother Charles took care of the Tucson operation, which advertised that its stock came direct from New York. Charles maintained the store until March 1873, when it abruptly closed and Charles moved to Las Cruces. By that time, Henry and his uncle had turned from merchandising to mining, becoming heavily involved in the development of copper mines in eastern Arizona.

Drachman's for a Good Smoke

About the same time that the Lesinskys appeared in Tucson, Hyman Goldberg's brother Isaac also located there. By 1867, he had been joined by Philip Drachman. Together these in-laws formed a general merchandise firm of Goldberg and Drachman. For the next decade, the business operated under that name as well as Goldberg and Company and Drachman and Company. Philip Drachman moved from dry goods in the 1870s to saloon keeping and finally acquired a cigar store, which he operated until his death in 1889.

Philip Drachman's younger brother Sam arrived in Tucson in September 1867. Sam claimed that reading journalist J. Ross Browne's descriptions of Arizona and its rich mines so "electrified" him that he booked passage on the next steamer for San Francisco. More likely, he was looking for work and his brother and other relatives already were living in the Southwest. At any rate, after visiting San Francisco, he sailed for the south coast. Landing at San Pedro, he made his way to San Bernardino, where he met up with Isaac Goldberg and began working for the family business. From San Bernardino, he joined a party heading for Arizona City (Yuma). There his journey was delayed when he was called on to serve for a few days as court

Tucson tobacconist Sam Drachman and his nephew Harry Arizona Drachman in front of Sam's store. *Courtesy Arizona Historical Society, #45530, Tucson, Arizona.*

clerk. He received no pay for his service, but after the trial, the judge did buy everyone a drink.

At last Sam boarded a stage for Tucson, but when the driver told him to be on the lookout for Apaches, he began questioning the wisdom of the trip: "To say the least, I felt as though I would rather be in Philadelphia and let someone else go in search of Arizona's wealth." At one point, he spied a cloud of dust in the distance, and he knew he was done for. Much to everyone's relief, however, the dust turned out to be a train of freight wagons belonging to Charles T. Hayden. Other than a snakebit mule, the remainder of the journey to Tucson proved uneventful, and when the stage finally arrived on September 4, 1867, Sam went right to work for Goldberg and Drachman. In 1873, Sam decided to strike out on his own. He established a modest but ultimately unsuccessful dry goods, clothing and grocery business. This setback, however, did not deter the ambitious young storekeeper. Within a year, Sam had recouped his losses and again had a small store selling general merchandise.

Sam left the general merchandise trade to become one of the town's favorite tobacconists in the 1880s. With the addition of a pool hall, his stand in the Wedge developed into a popular hangout for much of the male population through the end of the century.

Sam liked to advertise in the newspapers, and most of his ads were straightforward, if somewhat flowery:

> *Does your heart cry for rest*
> *In a place that is blest*
> *With no shadow or sorrow*
> *Nor care for tomorrow?*
> *Then go to Sam Drachman.*

Other advertisements were more subtle, as in a tale he probably placed in the *Arizona Weekly Citizen* in 1887 about a group of prospectors who returned to Tucson from the Santa Catalina Mountains with gold specimens. They had discovered

> *under an over hanging rock a vein of reddish decomposed quartz, full of gold. Some pieces were as large as one's open hand, and every specimen found was inscribed on one side, "always buy your cigars at Sam Drachman's, Tucson."*

On the other hand, the town's more faithful might have felt that Sam's humor in the "Ten Commandments" sign posted on the wall of the cigar store bordered on sacrilege. Some of the admonitions were:

I. Thou shalt have none other cigars to smoke than those kept by S.H. Drachman.

III. Thou salt not defraud, but shall pay unto S.H. Drachman that which is due.

IV. Thou shat not kiss, neither shalt thou make love to the hired girl in the absence of thy wife, but thou shalt buy cigars and tobacco of S.H. Drachman and live in peace.

V. Honor thy mother, and treat thy father to one of S.H. Drachman's Havana cigars.

IX. Love and honor thy mother-in-law. Go to S.H. Drachman's for thy cigars and be forever blessed.

Early in the following decade, Sam expanded his little tobacco empire to Phoenix. Sam's cigar stand had, indeed, become the stuff of legends, and he would continue as one of Tucson's most popular and colorful pioneer merchants until his death in 1911.

Jacob Mansfeld, Keeping Tucson Well Read

Arriving in the pueblo in 1869 was a Prussian Jew with quite a different idea of what to sell. Dry goods? No. Clothing? No. Groceries? No. Whiskey? Certainly not! Soon after coming to America, Jacob Mansfeld made his way west to the mining camps of California's Mother Lode country, where he became a merchant, later moving to Nevada and Idaho. Within a year of settling in Tucson, he had opened a newspaper, book and stationery store known as the Pioneer News Depot. Although southern Arizona was still very much on the frontier, Mansfeld later recalled that his customers were not of the wild and wooly variety. Rather, their tastes in literature inclined toward Charles Dickens and Alexandre Dumas, and not, "sensational and trashy reading."

Keeping his shelves stocked proved to be just as much a problem for Mansfeld as for the general merchants. It could take up to a month for newspapers and magazines to arrive from San Francisco or the East, and orders for the Christmas season might not appear until February. Since

"PIONEER NEWS DEPOT OF ARIZONA". PROPERTY OF J.S.MANSFELD, TUCSON, ARIZONA.
CORNER CONGRESS ST. AND WARNER ALLEY.

Above: For many years, Jacob Mansfeld's Pioneer News Depot kept Tucson readers and writers supplied with books, magazines, newspapers and stationery. *From History of Arizona Territory, 1884.*

Left: Besides operating his Pioneer News Depot, Jacob Mansfeld wrote Tucson's first city charter, established Arizona's first public library and served on the Territorial University's Board of Regents. *From History of Arizona Territory, 1884.*

many of his customers faced the same situation with their businesses, they understood, and the Pioneer News Depot became a local landmark of sorts and gathering place for the town's more intellectually inclined residents. It turned a profit as well. By 1885, Mansfeld estimated the value of the News Depot as at least $15,000. In order to drum up business and serve the community, in the early 1870s he started Tucson's first circulating library in a corner of the store. So popular did this become that by 1879 his library had grown to include reading matter in Spanish and German, reflecting the ethnicity of most of his clientele. Jacob Mansfeld never lost his interest in matters literary and scholarly. When the territorial legislature passed legislation creating the University of Arizona, he succeeded in convincing two of Tucson's leading gamblers and the owner of the town's foremost saloon to donate land for the institution. He also served on the first board of trustees of Tucson's public library and as a regent of the university. Mansfeld continued operating the Pioneer News Depot until his death in 1894.

Retailing in the Old Pueblo

The clothing business, including retail ready-to-wear, tailoring and millinery, was by far the most popular undertaking for Tucson's Jewish shopkeepers. After leaving William Zeckendorf, Theodore Welisch went on to establish the "Bazaar of Ladies Fashions," selling high-quality merchandise from eastern manufacturers. He also specialized in dressmaking and millinery, and to assist in these endeavors, he hired an employee who was thought to be Tucson's first female clerk. Theodore's brother Herman immigrated to the United States from Hungary in 1873. He located in Tucson and initially worked for L. Zeckendorf. Zeckendorf and Steinfeld set him up with a general store in the mill town of Charleston, where he made enough money to sell out and return to Hungary—but not for long. Herman soon returned to Arizona and joined Theodore in Tucson. For a while during the early 1880s, they operated Welisch Brothers Importing Business on South Main Street. About that time, Theodore and another partner, Leopold Wolf, also maintained a store called the White House, offering men's clothing and furnishing items as well as ladies apparel. The store prospered until January 1883, when Welisch & Wolf fell behind in their debts. Creditors, including the Levi Strauss Company, sued for payment. While Welisch blamed the failure on the unusually mild winter affecting the sale of seasonal goods, the excuse generated little sympathy and assignees sold all of the merchandise on hand. Wolf disappeared from Arizona, and Theodore went to work for Herman, who once again had a general store in Charleston.

Popular Jewish clothiers during the 1880s included Leo Goldschmidt's brother Adolph and his partner William Florsheim, who sold men's suits and furnishing goods. The partnership ended in 1885 when Goldschmidt decided to make a change and purchased a small grocery store. In three years, he transformed the grocery into a thriving wholesale company. While this was going on, Joseph Ferrin and Abraham Marx also sold clothes and engaged in tailoring at a store on Meyer Street until December 1883. At that time, the firm entered receivership. The partnership dissolved, and Marx left town. But because of his good reputation, creditors allowed Ferrin to remain in business as a merchant tailor. In 1887, he closed out the retail portion of this operation to devote himself full time to tailoring. Israel Gotthelf, Max and Emanuel Lowenstein and Jacob Harris also had clothing shops in Tucson, as did S.M. Seeligson and Isadore Meyer. The latter two stores were well patronized but went out of business when both of their proprietors retired in 1899. Through the end of the territorial period, Tucsonans patronized Jewish clothiers, including Bernard Rosenfeld, Fred Borenstein, Adolph Levy and Sol Ryttenberg.

For many years, Fred Fleishman supplied Tucson with medicines and other merchandise. *Courtesy Arizona Jewish Historical Society, Phoenix, Arizona.*

The demand for mining implements and hardware in southern Arizona prompted Morris Wolf and Marcus Katz to be both partners and competitors during the late nineteenth century. From the 1870s through the early twentieth century, German Jew Fred Fleishman was the town's leading druggist, or at least he advertised himself as such. Jews in the grocery business included A. Goodman, Carl Seligman and Max Zeir. While their stores may not have been large, they provided the town with staples and delicacies, as well as serving as outlets for produce from truck farms in the area. The arrival of the railroad also meant that ice could be imported, enabling these grocers to offer a wider variety of perishable goods to compete with the larger general merchandise houses.

Jews had been involved in the jewelry trade since the days of the Renaissance, if not before. It was not surprising, therefore, that they brought such knowledge and skills to Tucson. In the 1890s, Aaron Zeckendorf's son Hugo opened a jewelry store on the corner of Main and Congress Streets. There he sold rings, diamonds, necklaces and stickpins. He also manufactured watches to order, sold spectacles and even rented pianos. Slow business, probably caused by the depression of 1893, however, compelled him to close and then lease space in his uncle Louis's dry goods building. This arrangement lasted but a few years when relations with Louis became strained. Hugo closed and moved with his family to San Francisco. Early in the following decade, Morris Gruenwald opened his Tucson jewelry store. In 1906, he took in partner Fred Adams, establishing the long-lasting firm of Gruenwald and Adams.

Leo Goldschmidt became Tucson's leading furniture dealer beginning in the late 1870s. He imported wagon and later boxcar loads of chairs, tables, mirrors, beds, chests, bureaus and other items from eastern and Pacific coast manufacturers, proudly displaying them in a showroom on the corner of Meyer and Jackson Streets. In May 1882, however, a fire destroyed a considerable amount of the inventory. While they could not save the building, firemen and passersby worked valiantly to carry out as much merchandise as possible. Nevertheless, between $35,000 and $40,000 worth of furniture had been consumed, with insurance not even covering half of the loss. Fortunately, Leo had some "reserve stock" housed in an off-site warehouse, enabling him to reopen in a new location. In 1888, Leo disposed of his furniture business to L. Zeckendorf & Company and went on to operate the Eagle Flour mill and pursue his fortune in banking.

"Boss Levin"

After arriving in Tucson from La Paz, Alexander Levin initially partnered with Frank Hodges in the Pioneer Brewery. This arrangement lasted for about three years, after which he bought out his partner. Alexander joined with another Prussian Jew, liquor dealer Joseph Goldtree, in a brewery that advertised lager beer, ale and porter, as well as luncheon delicacies including Swiss cheese, herring, anchovies and potato salad.

By 1873, the partnership with Goldtree had ended, but Alexander now had a new partner, his wife, Zenona Molina, from Hermosillo Sonora. Together they opened the Park Brewery at the foot of Pennington Street. In addition to the usual porters and ales, the Park Brewery manufactured sarsaparilla and soda water. As he had at La Paz, Alexander also set up a free public bathhouse near the brewery and acquired a hotel as well as a number of saloons around town to serve as outlets for his beer. A beer garden adjoined the brewery, as did a three-acre fenced park. The owners invited Tucsonans to visit and "bring their families without any fear of meeting disrespectful parties on the grounds, as none will be allowed there." Eventually shaded by eucalyptus, pepper, cottonwood and fruit trees carefully planted by Alexander and Zenona, the park came to feature flower and vegetable gardens, a restaurant, dancing pavilion, billiard tables, croquet green, shooting gallery and archery range, bowling alley and roller-skating rink. By the mid-1870s, Alexander had become known as "Boss Levin," and his park became the site of the Fiesta de San Agustin as well as other community events.

In 1878, Alexander also constructed Park Hall near the site. As the pueblo's first formal theater, it hosted a number of road show companies and light operas. So popular were his developments that the press noted, "The people of Tucson could hardly do without Levin's Park." After a decade and a half of hard work, the Levins seemed to have it made.

The arrival of the Southern Pacific Railroad in Tucson in March 1880 had a significant effect on Alexander and his beer. Although the civic-minded Boss served proudly on the celebration committee and hosted a banquet at the park to honor the iron horse, it was not long before the trains brought cold beer from California and the East at prices that could not be matched. As a result, the Levins leased the brewery and concentrated on mining and other investments (usually unprofitable) and civic activities. In 1887, after some financial difficulties, they moved to Mexico.

Alexander and Zenona returned to Tucson four years later. By this time, however, the park had been eclipsed by Carrillo's Gardens, a newer, larger

Levin's Park, for many years Tucson's center for social events, recreation and beer. *Courtesy Arizona Historical Society, #14848, Tucson, Arizona.*

and more elaborate entertainment and recreation venue. (It even featured a zoo.) The neighborhoods surrounding the two locations also may have had something to do with the park's decline. While Levin's Park occupied land near the downtown area, Carrillo's was in a more "suburban" district favored by many of Tucson's business and civic leaders. Visitation declined, and the park began attracting some of the seedier elements of Tucson society. As early as 1884, the *Arizona Daily Star* commented that the park had outlived its usefulness to the community. The park struggled through the remainder of the decade, occasionally hosting special events and parties. Alexander tried to spruce things up when he returned, but the Boss's death from a heart attack in 1891 signaled the end of Tucson's first brewery and amusement park.

Selim Franklin and the University

Like many other brothers in the territory, Abe and Selim Franklin were as different as different could be. Descended from a prosperous family of English Jews, they were nephews of Lionel and Barron Jacobs. The elder, Abe, found his place in frontier towns, where as a young man he hobnobbed with cowboys and outlaws. They called him the "Kid." More about him later. Selim, on the other hand, was more at home in the halls of justice. A graduate of the University of California and admitted to the California Bar, he moved to Arizona and settled in Tucson. He served as city attorney and was elected in 1884 to the Thirteenth Territorial Legislature. The Thirteenth did not have a particularly stellar reputation. Nevertheless, largely through Selim's efforts, the body enacted legislation creating the University of Arizona. Franklin later recalled that his flowery oratory played on the consciences of his fellow politicians:

> *I told my associates that it was conceded that the 13th Legislature was the most energetic, the most contentious and the most corrupt legislature that Arizona had had. We were called the fighting thirteenth, the bloody thirteenth, the thieving thirteenth, and we deserved those names; and we all knew it. We had employed so many clerks for our committees that each member had one and a half clerks. We had subsidized the local press with extravagant appropriations so that our shortcomings should not be published in their columns; we had voted ourselves additional pay in violation of the Act of Congress.*
>
> *"But, gentlemen," I said, "here is an opportunity to wash away our sins. Let us establish an institution of learning; let us pass this bill creating a University, where for all time to come the youth of this land may have opportunities of education; where they may learn to be better citizens than we are; and all our shortcomings will be forgotten in a misty past, and we will be remembered for this one great achievement."*

The lawmakers responded enthusiastically. Perhaps out of a sense of guilt, perhaps to improve their reputations, they passed the bill. For his role in establishing the school, Selim Franklin gained the title "Father of the Arizona University," which he kept until his sudden death in November 1927.

5

JEWS WHERE YOU LEAST EXPECT THEM

WHEN NOGALES WAS ISAACSON

The border between Arizona and the Mexican state of Sonora runs some 365 miles. Until the late nineteenth century, it was largely unmarked and uninhabited. Eventually, a number of towns and ranches would be established along the international line. The largest would be Nogales—but it was not always known as Nogales.

Located on both sides of the border, the town developed into a major port of entry and trading center for Americans and Mexicans. In 1880, the Atchison, Topeka and Santa Fe Railway began construction of a line from the Mexican port of Guaymas north to the United States. The place where it would connect with tracks being built from Deming, New Mexico, was first called Line City. There the locomotives of the American and Mexican railroads changed and new crews were assigned. This activity meant people, and people meant money.

In 1880, Jacob Isaacson and his older brother Isaac, from Russian Poland, arrived in Tucson, where they scratched out a living as peddlers. Sensing a business opportunity, they journeyed south to open a one-room adobe trading post on the border. Their only neighbors were a Mexican roadhouse and customs office. The brothers' patrons included railroad workers, wagon freighters, soldiers, ranchers, miners and occasionally outlaws. Isaac departed soon after the post's establishment, leaving Jacob on his own. He later recalled how it felt to be by himself:

It was lonely in those times, yes very lonely. On some days there would be little or no travel and during the nights I had only the stars to keep me company. On top of all of this solitude the Apaches were still in the land and always there existed the awful dread that they would come in the dead of night and with the rising sun, and would find me unprepared to fight for my life. More than one visit did I get from them, but I always managed to get away with my life.

Jacob may have exaggerated a bit, but not much. Apaches did pass frequently through the region on their raids, as did cattle rustlers and smugglers. On those lonely evenings he also may have reminisced about his youth in the old country when he studied to become a rabbi.

Jacob's isolation eased somewhat, and a little settlement that developed around the trading post became known as Isaacson. Jacob served as its postmaster. Isaacson remained on the postal service's books until 1883, when the town was renamed Nogales because of the many walnut trees that grew in the pass. The two railroads met on October 25, 1882, and Jacob was present at the ceremony. By this time, his trading post had been joined by tent and clapboard saloons, restaurants, boardinghouses and stores. For a short time, business was good, but within a year, once the railroad excitement subsided, the brothers had closed their store. Jacob left for Mexico and Isaac for Los Angeles. Jacob later operated stores in California, Oregon, Missouri and Texas. After his second wife deserted him, taking all of his worldly goods, a severely depressed Jacob went to live with his sister in Detroit. He occasionally returned to visit Arizona but never fully recovered his mental faculties, dying in a Michigan asylum in 1928. Isaac became a pawnbroker and spent his last days running a secondhand shop in San Francisco.

Jacob Isaacson (*above*) and his brother Isaac established a trading post on the Mexican border. Called Isaacson, the settlement grew into the town of Nogales. *Courtesy Arizona Historical Society, #7855, Tucson, Arizona.*

The Fat Jew and Other Entrepreneurs on the Border

The departure of the Isaacsons did not end Jewish involvement in Nogales. They were just the beginning. Nineteen-year-old Leopold Ephraim left his native Prussian Poland for the United States in 1869. After living in the South, he moved to Montana, where he became a peddler, traveling throughout the region in a wagon clanking with pots and pans. He also invested in some mines, which turned a tidy profit. He married, but his young bride died a short time later. Maybe Montana now held too many bad memories, or maybe his business had begun to decline, or both, but Leopold went next to San Francisco, where he became a restaurateur and stock speculator. Neither of these endeavors turned out well, and by the late 1870s, he was broke. Hearing of mining strikes in Arizona, he decided his luck could not get any worse and headed for the territory. Unfortunately, he could not afford passage, or even a horse, so he took off on foot. Dusty, footsore and even more broke, he arrived in Tucson and looked up an old acquaintance, Albert Steinfeld. The sympathetic merchant saw beyond Leopold's shabby appearance and advanced him credit on some merchandise as well as transportation to Tubac. There he opened a tent store, using flour and sugar sacks to erect a makeshift fort to protect himself from Apache raiders. But no raiders came, and Leopold actually started making money.

While the Tubac store enabled Leopold Ephraim to get on his feet again, it was a sleepy village, not a place for a young man to make his fortune. Like the Isaacsons, he saw potential in the border crossing to the south. By 1882, he had relocated to a rude plank and canvas store on Morley Street in what would be Nogales. Along with Jacob Isaacson, he was present at the completion of the railroad, but unlike Jacob and Isaac, he would become a fixture in the new community. By the mid-1880s, he had built a more permanent building and was said to possess the largest stock of general merchandise in town. Leopold did so well in Nogales that he ventured into a number of other fields, including ownership of the profitable El Promontorio silver mine in Sonora. He also purchased large tracts of land, some of which he donated to the City of Nogales as a public cemetery, and developed the Nogales Water Company. As his business interests expanded, so did his waistline, and eventually he began calling himself the "Fat Jew." In 1909, Leopold traveled to Europe, returning with a Jewish wife. Because of a respiratory condition, however, his new bride could not live at Nogales's almost four-thousand-foot elevation, so the couple moved permanently to Los Angeles, where Leopold died in 1923.

In the waning years of the nineteenth century, other Jews engaged in business on both sides of the international line. Before moving to Phoenix in the early 1890s, William Melczer had a general merchandise and liquor business serving southern Arizona and northern Sonora. Brothers Louis and Richard Fleischer became well-known tailors in American and Mexican Nogales. In 1895, they purchased a clothing business previously owned by M.G. Levy and Ben Goldsmith, thereby establishing themselves as the largest retail clothiers south of Tucson. A little ways away, amid a haze of fragrant aromas, Richard Fleischer partnered in August 1898 with William Shuckmann in a cigar factory. There they produced the "Dos Naciones" brand, one of turn-of-the-century Arizona's most popular smokes. Other Jewish businessmen, probably enjoying a Dos Naciones from time to time, might have been tailor William Rosenberg, aka "Rosie the Tailor"; general merchant Fred Borenstein, proprietor of the El Paso Store; or maybe L. Rosenstern and B. Schwab of the Peoples' Store.

THE MAYOR SITS DOWN WITH (OR AT LEAST CLOSE TO) GERONIMO

On March 27, 1886, General George Crook, along with some soldiers and civilians, met to talk peace with the Chiricahua Apache leader Geronimo in the remote Canon de los Embudos in the Sierra Madre of Sonora. Tombstone photographer Camillus S. Fly captured a classic image of the meeting. Crook, wearing his trademark pith helmet, and Geronimo, with Warm Springs Apache chief Nana, are easily discernable. But off to the side, sharing a perch with some Apaches and peering down through the bushes at the proceeding, is a bearded civilian, Charles Moses Strauss, a Jew and the former mayor of Tucson. One of the few nonmilitary personnel Crook allowed to accompany his expedition into Mexico, Strauss was one of the best-known Jews in Arizona and had become a friend of the general. He had a sense of history, and this would be a historic meeting.

Strauss was born in 1840 in New York City and educated in Boston, attending both public and Hebrew schools. After working as a clerk, he moved to Memphis, Tennessee, and there he engaged in business and married Julia Kaufman. The Strausses moved to Massachusetts in 1870, where Charles ran unsuccessfully for secretary of state. Repeated bouts of tuberculosis prompted the family to relocate to southern Arizona's dry climate in 1880. He found employment with L. Zeckendorf and oversaw construction of

Geronimo and General George Crook discuss surrender in Canyon de los Embudos. In bushes to the right, Tucson mayor Charles M. Strauss observes. *Courtesy Arizona State Library, Archives and Public Records, History and Archives Division, #97-2621, Phoenix.*

the firm's new building. He also joined the volunteer fire department and the school board. The Strauss home became a center for social and literary activities in Tucson. Julia hosted the first meeting of the Lotus Club, a social and cultural organization made up largely of Jewish women.

In 1883, Charles ran for mayor. When his opponent tried to capitalize on the fact that he was a Jew, the *Arizona Star* newspaper countered, "We shall elect Mr. Strauss mayor, Jew and all." And they did. Mayor Strauss had some big ideas for his adopted town. He organized the celebration for General Crook, arranging both a theatrical performance and banquet at Levin's Park. Despite an adversarial relationship with the council, he succeeded in starting a program of street grading and getting a new city hall, municipal infirmary and public library built. When he tried floating a bond issue to pay for the improvements, the Pima County grand jury deemed the act illegal. The charges were thrown out, but on August 8, 1884, Charles resigned following the unanimous overturning of his veto of a council resolution he felt undermined his authority. The council accepted his resignation without regret.

Charles's resignation, however, did not end his public service. He was appointed to the Board of Regents of the new University of Arizona and in 1886 won election as territorial superintendent of public instruction. He fought to uphold the office's authority and encouraged the construction of more schools in rural districts. He also founded and served as first president of the Territorial Teachers' Association, which upheld standards for public school instructors. Although Strauss's detractors called him a "fossiliferous old fraud," when the position became appointed, Governor Conrad Zulick chose Strauss, who stayed until 1889. He served as clerk of the Sixteenth Territorial Legislature in 1891 and director of Tucson's School District Number One. By the following year, however, he was ill with a recurrence of tuberculosis. Charles Moses Strauss died on March 13, 1892, at the age of fifty-two. On the day of his funeral, the town's schools and some of its businesses closed as a measure of respect.

Jews on the Big Sandy

During the territorial era, few places in Arizona were as remote as the Big Sandy River valley in the northwest. With oppressive summer heat and rains that could wash out roads in an instant, the Big Sandy country did not attract many settlers. From the 1870s to the 1930s, the region's principal settlement was the gold and silver mining town of Signal. Hardly a metropolis or even a boomtown, it nonetheless boasted three restaurants, thirteen saloons and a brewery. The town also had merchants, two of whom were Jewish, brothers Moise (or Moses, or Mose as he liked to be called) and Gabriel "Gabe" Levy. The Levy brothers migrated to the United States from the Alsace and for some reason wound up in Signal. They operated a general store, ran some cattle and developed a few mines. Mose also served for a time as Signal's justice of the peace, known for his stiff sentences. The Levy brothers partnered in the store with their cousins Henry and William Koshland, who also migrated from the Alsace to Signal in the early 1870s. The Koshlands ran cattle along the Big Sandy and did some mining. Henry Koshland became one of the region's most prominent citizens, dabbling in politics until his death in 1896 from a blood infection after being stuck by a mesquite thorn. William Koshland eventually returned to Germany. Mose retired to San Francisco, where he passed away in 1904. Gabe, on the other hand, remained in Signal during the community's long decline. He became postmaster, justice of the peace and even a weather reporter for Phoenix's

Gabriel Levy's store in Signal, Arizona. An older Levy is on the far right. *Courtesy Mohave Museum of History and the Arts, Kingman, Arizona.*

Arizona Republican newspaper. He died in Kingman in January 1932 at age seventy-seven. Mose and Gabe Levy and Henry Koshland had their bodies shipped to Colma, California, and buried in the Home of Peace Cemetery and Emanu-El Mausoleum. Also ranching in the Big Sandy country during this time were Isaac Goodman, known as a stock king of the region, and Charles Cohen, who abandoned his career as a Prescott storekeeper to become a full-time cattle raiser in the remote valley.

THE SCHUSTERS OF HOLBROOK

Early in 1884, Jewish twin brothers Adolf and Ben Schuster showed up on the muddy and cold streets of Holbrook, a Wild West cow town on the main line of the Atlantic and Pacific Railroad in northeastern Arizona. At that time, Holbrook had a less than savory reputation. Populated largely by cowboys, sheepmen, rustlers, outlaws, saloonkeepers, railroaders and the occasional farmer, it was known as, historian Harold Wayte stated, "the town too tough for women and churches." But it was not too tough for the brothers Schuster. Born in Westphalia, Germany, in 1862, Adolf and Ben had come to the United States in 1878 and 1880, respectively, and lived in Santa Fe, El Paso and the Mexican state of Chihuahua prior to Arizona. Despite Holbrook's rough appearance, they decided that it would be a

Adolf and Ben Schuster's Holbrook Store rebuilt after a fire in 1888. It was located between the "Bucket of Blood" saloon tent and the Mormon Arizona Cooperative Mercantile Institution store. *Courtesy A&B Schuster Collection, Museum of Northern Arizona, Flagstaff, Arizona.*

good place to locate a general merchandise store. After all, even outlaws had to wear clothes and eat. With savings from their work in Mexico, they purchased inventory and set up shop in what was little more than a shack. The brothers lived in the back room. A prominent sign over the front door read, "A. and B. Schuster Company."

The brothers soon were major suppliers to Anglo and Hispanic ranchers in northeastern Arizona and western New Mexico. In 1900, another brother, Max, joined them to run the company's dry goods department. The Schusters also became wagon freighters, competing successfully with Mormon teamsters for traffic in the Little Colorado River valley. On the return trips to Holbrook, the Schusters transported farm and ranch products to the railroad. Both directions turned a profit.

In 1891, the A. and B. Schuster Company expanded to include a branch at St. John's on the Little Colorado River, and five years later another store was opened at Whiteriver on the Fort Apache Indian Reservation. A third branch was located at the ranching hamlet of Concho, about fifteen miles west of St. John's. In addition to merchandising, the Schusters maintained large flocks of sheep from the Navajo Indian Reservation all the way down to Cave Creek in Maricopa County. Adolf and Ben arranged their schedules so that one would mind the main store in Holbrook, while the other oversaw management of the sheep and checked on branch operations. They became active in the Arizona Woolgrowers Association and for many years owned or leased cattle ranches in Apache County. Ben Schuster eventually moved to St. John's on the Little Colorado River. He died in 1911. Adolf retired to Los Angeles, where he passed away in 1934.

Jews among the Saints—the Barths

Sol Barth, employee of Michel Goldwater, mail contractor, expressman, trader and freighter, moved from central Arizona to the Little Colorado River region in the early 1870s. He already had a sullied reputation resulting from the alleged sham gold robbery in 1864, but in remote eastern Arizona that hardly mattered. Along with brothers Nathan, Isaac and Morris and some New Mexican workers they located at El Vadito, a crossing of the Little Colorado. There Sol began diverting water to irrigate farmland. In 1873, according to legend, Sol won a poker game with some Mexican ranchers, receiving land and cattle. The brothers put the cows to pasture and established the town of St. John's on the land, replacing El Vadito. They also opened a general merchandise business serving neighboring farmers and herdsmen.

Mormon colonists were beginning to populate the region, and Sol could see that they would soon dominate ranching and farming around St. John's. He therefore sold them his extensive farming properties, once again receiving livestock as payment. Over the next decade, the Barth family enterprises expanded to include a hotel at St. John's and stores in Holbrook, Winslow and Flagstaff. By 1890, however, Sol had sold off the mercantile operations to concentrate on sheep raising.

Success in business and livestock led to the Barths' involvement in local and territorial politics. In 1879, Sol and his sometime associate Gentile Albert Franklin Banta successfully lobbied the legislature to create Apache County separate from Yavapai, with St. John's as the county seat. Sol became the first councilman in the legislature from the new county. From his expansive adobe home, he also controlled who would be elected or appointed offices in the county and had considerable influence among Hispanic voters. In 1887, Sol served briefly as county treasurer, an office that would land him in some hot water. In 1884, brother Morris was elected to the long term as Apache County supervisor, but he lost his life in a train accident prior to taking his seat.

There is no doubt that by the time Sol Barth sold out to the Mormons, the family was the wealthiest and most powerful clan in the Little Colorado River region. Nevertheless, they just could not seem to keep out of trouble, particularly Sol. As early as 1868, rumors had him illegally trading guns, powder and lead to the Apaches. Of course, he professed innocence and the charge went away. The 1870s and 1880s were particularly troublesome for the Barths. In April 1874, a grand jury for New Mexico's Second Judicial District in Santa Fe charged Sol with stealing two government mules. In September and the following year, two subpoenas were issued against Sol for larceny, claiming that he had been selling liquor without paying special taxes. Also in 1875, the Tucson *Arizona Citizen* reported that Sol had killed a man along the Little Colorado above Fort Apache. Nothing came of any of these accusations. But where there was smoke…

Things did not get any better for the Barths in the 1880s. In 1884, they were having business troubles with the firm of Z. Staab & Company of New Mexico. They owed quite a bit of money, and a warrant went out for Sol's arrest. When he took the train to Albuquerque, allegedly to sort things out with the Staabs, he got off on the opposite side of the coach to avoid lawmen waiting for him on the platform. Eventually, Sol was caught and jailed until he could arrange matters with his creditors. The following year, he was arrested on a count of perjury stemming from another legal case in which he was involved. Interestingly, the sheriff of Yavapai County made the pinch because the Apache County sheriff refused to do so. Once again he escaped prosecution. Evidently, Sol still had quite a bit of clout in his home county.

Also in 1884, Nathan Barth found his way into jail as the result of a violent scuffle between Sol and Albert Banta at a hotel in St. John's. Barth and Banta had been on again, off again friends, but this day they were definitely off. A verbal confrontation got out of hand, and Sol grabbed his opponent by the neck but soon was getting the worst of it. Banta poked him repeatedly with a penknife, and Sol shouted to his brother that he would be killed. Nathan pulled his revolver and fired. The bullet passed through Sol's hand and into Banta's neck. Banta yanked and aimed his new double-action pistol at Nathan, but it did not fire. The sheriff then stepped in and broke up the fracas. Both Sol and Banta recovered. Banta spent some time in jail, but in the end, it was Nathan who faced assault charges. The jury, however, found him not guilty since the shooting was not premeditated and he was defending his family.

Up until the mid-1880s, Sol Barth had been able to avoid serious jail time for his indiscretions. Sometimes he was found not guilty; on other occasions, he discovered legal loopholes or engaged in a little bribery to make the charges go away. But that was about to change. In 1886, rumors circulated that as county treasurer he had doctored Apache County financial records to conceal forgery of county warrants to raise their value to much more than their original face amount. Why Sol would have done so is still a question. The likeliest reason is that the warrants were part of a speculative scheme in which he had become involved. At least that is what the district attorney argued. Unable to wiggle out of this predicament, Sol faced trial. Nathan tried to get his brother off by bribing jurors but instead was caught and fined $500. Without his "support network," Sol was convicted and received ten years in the territorial prison.

On April 28, 1887, he became Yuma Prison convict no. 442—height 5'3", light complexion, brown hair and blue eyes. Not long after entering prison, Sol again found himself embroiled in controversy. Barth's enemies charged that the warden gave him preferential treatment because the two had been friends since their days together in the territorial legislature. The warden immediately denied the accusation, claiming that he had never served in the legislature and that he and Sol weren't friends. Barth received the same treatment as the other prisoners.

Sol appealed his conviction to the territorial supreme court, but lost. A movement among his supporters began to convince Governor Zulick to issue him a pardon. All of the jurors at his trial signed a petition to that effect, as did over four hundred citizens. Territorial newspapers opined that Sol had probably been railroaded. Finally, on March 12, 1889, the governor issued a pardon and ordered his release.

Even though Sol had served only two years, many Arizonans felt he would emerge from Yuma a broken man. They were wrong. He quickly regained economic and political control of the St. John's region and even sued to recover money he had lost during the county warrants scandal. In 1896, just about ten years after his felony conviction, Apache County voters sent Sol to the council of the Nineteenth Territorial Legislature.

Sol Barth continued to be active in Apache County business and political affairs well into the twentieth century, but with fewer controversies. He died in 1928 and at his request had his funeral in the Mormon Church. With Sol's death passed one of the most colorful, and certainly controversial, Jews of the territorial era.

SOLOMONS OF SOLOMONVILLE

When Anna Solomon, a member of the prominent Freudenthal family of southern New Mexico, recalled coming to Arizona in 1876, she shuddered, "I did not expect to get here alive with our children." Indian ambush was always on her mind. Anna and her husband, Isadore, were both born in

Gila River Valley pioneers Isadore and Anna Solomon. *Courtesy Arizona Jewish Historical Society, Phoenix, Arizona.*

Isadore and Anna Solomon's general store prior to the establishment of the Commercial Company and hotel. *Courtesy Arizona State Library, Archives and Public Records, #97-8473, Phoenix.*

Posen. As a young man of eighteen, Isadore came to the United States with an uncle in 1858 and settled in Towanda, Pennsylvania. There he established a livery business and became a U.S. citizen. Isadore returned to Europe in 1871 to visit his parents and met and courted Anna. They married and soon after came to America, settling first in Towanda. Profits from the livery business, however, began declining, and in 1876 at the urging of the Freudenthals, they sold all they had and with their three children traveled by train and stagecoach to Dona Ana County. After living in Mesilla for four months, Isadore could not find suitable employment. He finally took a job in the Clifton/Morenci copper mines of eastern Arizona. One day on an outing, he spotted the Gila River valley, rich with mesquite trees. At that time, the mines needed high-quality charcoal to fuel the furnaces. Isadore entered into a contract with the mine owners, Anna's uncle Julius Freudenthal and cousins Charles and Henry Lesinsky, to burn mesquite and haul the charcoal to Clifton/Morenci. Isadore then loaded the family on a buckboard and headed for Pueblo Viejo, where about five Mexican families eked out a living in the Gila valley. There the Solomons would make their headquarters.

One charcoal contract followed another and allowed the Solomons to establish a mercantile business in Solomonville (as Pueblo Viejo came to be known). As more and more mesquite trees were removed, Isadore also expanded into agriculture and livestock raising. Eventually, he came to own some 1,300 acres of land as well as irrigation canals. At first, Anna looked after a general store in a small adobe. Eventually, with his brother Adolph and a Quaker by the name of David Wickersham, Solomon developed the store into a two-story building constructed of lumber from Mount Graham and firebrick brought from El Paso. It had wood floors and cherry and hardwood interiors, shelves and counters. The second story became a favorite gathering place for the growing population of the Gila valley. In addition to the general merchandise store and warehouse at Solomonville, the firm maintained a branch at Bowie Station on the Southern Pacific Railroad, a stagecoach line, freight wagons and a flour mill.

The 1890s proved difficult for Isadore Solomon and his partners. The national depression of 1893 placed a number of farmers and ranchers in jeopardy. This, in turn, affected Isadore, who carried their accounts. At the same time, the mines at Clifton/Morenci were hit hard by the economic slump. Since Isadore had considerable business dealings with the mines, this weakened his financial position. A problem also surfaced with completion in 1898 of the Gila Valley, Globe and Northern Railway from Bowie Station to the copper camp of Globe. Although Isadore was a director of the railroad, engineering considerations caused its tracks to bypass Solomonville in favor of the nearby community of Safford. Safford's growth would accelerate while Solomonville risked becoming a backwater.

The Solomon Commercial Company building dominated the town of Solomonville. *Courtesy Arizona Jewish Historical Society, Phoenix, Arizona.*

Interior of a country store in territorial Arizona. The Solomon Commercial Company in the late nineteenth century. *Courtesy Arizona Jewish Historical Society, Phoenix, Arizona.*

The solution to both problems came in 1899 when Morenci businessman H.G. Van Gorder and promoter A.G. Smith suggested to Isadore that a bank be organized. The Solomon store had for some time been making loans and storing money and other valuables. The new bank would be organized to assist agricultural, mining and mercantile interests on a more professional basis. Isadore proved receptive to the idea, and in 1899, he headed a group consisting of the Solomon family, Wickersham and some close business colleagues in the incorporation of the Solomon Commercial Company and Gila Valley Bank, with headquarters in the Solomonville store. Of the fourteen original investors, six were Solomon family members or relatives who held 152 of the bank's original 250 shares. The bank purchased the accounts of the Commercial Company and handled collections, thereby putting the mercantile operation on a more stable financial footing.

The death of Adolph Solomon and the decision of Isadore's son Charles to pursue banking elsewhere led Isadore, Wickersham and the original investors to withdraw from the company in 1908. The Solomons, however, continued to be interested in Arizona banking, with Charles becoming president of Tucson's Arizona National Bank.

By the 1910s, the Solomons had cut back their business activities considerably. The Commercial Company was sold in 1916 and the hotel three years later. In the 1920s, Anna and Isadore retired to a more comfortable life in Los Angeles. Anna relished the sophisticated environment in California—Isadore, ever the frontiersman, not so much. He passed away there in 1930, as did Anna in 1933.

DR. HERMAN BENDELL AMONG THE INDIANS

Herman Bendell was the son of pioneers. His parents, Elias and Hannah Bendell, were among the first Jews to settle in Albany, New York. He pursued a career in medicine and served as a surgeon in the Union army. After the war, President Ulysses S. Grant adopted a "Peace Policy" with Native Americans on the frontier. At first, Quaker agents were sent west, but Simon Wolf, a friend of the president, suggested Dr. Bendell. Despite criticism from the eastern press and religious leaders that the doctor was not a Christian, Grant went ahead and appointed him as superintendent of Indian affairs for the Arizona Territory.

Bendell arrived in Arizona 1871, just after the infamous Camp Grant Massacre at which a band Tohono O'odham Indians, Mejicanos and a few Anglo-American ringleaders attacked a settlement of Aravaipa Apaches living under supposed army protection. They killed 144, mostly women and children, and captured more for sale into slavery. Shocked by this atrocity, Bendell spent his time traveling about the territory, visiting the reservations, urging reforms and writing to convince the federal government (not always successfully) to deal peacefully with the Indians.

Neither the military and their suppliers nor traders with the Indians, who often were Jewish themselves, liked Bendell. General George Crook accused him of embezzling tens of thousands of dollars during his tenure in Arizona but offered no proof. Newspaperman and historian Abraham Chanin summed up reasons for Bendell's brief tenure in Arizona. He was just "too fair, too honest, and too Jewish." Church leaders argued that the superintendent's position should be held by a Christian who could serve as missionary as well as administrator. They finally prevailed. Before departing Arizona, the doctor did invest in a mine but did not become rich. He resigned his position in 1873, going on to serve briefly as a U.S. consul in Denmark and then enjoying a long and distinguished medical career. He died in Albany in 1932 at the age of eighty-nine.

6

HARDROCK MINERS AND HARDCASH MERCHANTS

Gold and silver brought the first substantial numbers of Jews to Arizona. Some prospected, at least for a while. Others grubstaked miners and invested in mines. Most sold supplies and provisions that miners eagerly purchased. Before the arrival of banks, their stores also were seen as safe places to deposit their nuggets and dust. Jews became integral members of the mining communities who dedicated their time, effort and money in developing the territory's mineral wealth. But just who were they?

MAKING MONEY AT THE VULTURE MINE

Prospector Henry Wickenburg, who was not Jewish, discovered the Vulture Mine in the desert hills northwest of the Salt River valley in 1863. He realized that it had the potential to be a major gold producer but lacked the resources to exploit his find. A steam-powered mill that could pulverize ore and efficiently separate the gold and silver from the waste rock would do the trick. Such a mill, however, cost a lot of money and would have to be transported in parts from San Francisco then reassembled on site. Wickenburg and his initial partners did not have the financial wherewithal to acquire such machinery. But merchants in the territory did. Perhaps an arrangement could be made by which these storekeepers could front the money for the new equipment, with the owners paying them back from the profits.

In 1866, two of the biggest merchants in the region were partners Bernard Cohn and Mike Goldwater of La Paz. The Vulture Mine owners, therefore, approached them with a proposal to erect a modern ore-processing facility. Once the mill began operation, the mine owners would repay the debt. Sensing an opportunity, Goldwater and Cohn agreed. Mike trudged off to San Francisco, bringing with him a mining expert to make sure he got the best machinery at the best price. They ended up buying a twenty-stamp mill and processing equipment and had it shipped around Baja California to the Colorado River and on to the mine.

Once back in Arizona, however, the arrangement with the owners got off to a rocky start. Payment was slow in coming. Something had to be done. Mike met with the owners to sort things out, and they agreed that the debt amounted to about $35,000 at 2 percent per month. The parties came to an arrangement by which Goldwater and Cohn would, in effect, become temporary owners of the Vulture and receive all of the proceeds from the mine until the debt was satisfied. It was a gamble. If the rock continued to contain high concentrations of gold and silver, Cohn and Goldwater could realize a tidy profit. If not, then their money would be wasted.

The ore from the Vulture proved to be richer than expected, and within three months the money owed for the stamp mill and equipment had been paid back. Thanks largely to their investment, the Vulture was well on its way to becoming one of the most important producers in the territory. But this did not end Mike Goldwater's association with the mine. The Vulture Mine would yield thousands of ounces of gold and silver, and J. Goldwater & Bro. continued to sell the company and its employees considerable amounts of supplies. Income from this arrangement helped fund the Goldwaters' commercial expansion in Arizona well beyond the Colorado River.

Tombstone Characters

Tombstone—no other location in Territorial Arizona reflected its Wild West reputation more than did this Cochise County silver mining boomtown. And no other town remains as legendary as the "Town Too Tough to Die." Founded in 1879, by the mid-1880s, its glory days had passed. But in the interim, Tombstone boasted colorful residents, including the Earp brothers; Doc Holliday and his sometime consort, "Big Nose Kate"; gunman "Buckskin Frank" Leslie; and restaurateur Nellie Cashman, the "miners' angel." Along with these came some less savory settlers living nearby: the Clanton clan,

Allen Street, Tombstone's principal commercial thoroughfare, in 1880. Martin Calisher's general store is on the right, a few blocks from the OK Corral. *Courtesy Arizona Historical Society, #14835, Tucson, Arizona.*

"Curly Bill" Brocius and the "Cowboys." Crime usually consisted of high-spirited miners or cowboys trying to rearrange some of the livelier parts of town. Serious violence involved liquor, gambling, politics and women and ended up with one of the parties dead or injured and the other in jail.

During Tombstone's halcyon years, Jews took a leading role in the commercial life of the community. At least seventy-five Jewish families, as well as a number of single men, settled in the mining town. At first, they operated general merchandise houses. Their stores fronted on Allen and Fremont Streets, dusty during dry periods, muddy when it rained and filled with manure and garbage almost all the time. Prominent among these early storekeepers were Phoenix and Tucson merchants Hyman Goldberg, Rudolph Cohen, M.H. Seligman and B. Laventhal, whose Miners and Mechanics Store suggested its customer base. Also coming to Tombstone from Florence at this time was Martin Calisher, brother-in-law of Lionel and Barron Jacobs. At his Allen Street business, Calisher and his son David sold general merchandise and lumber along with building materials—necessary items in a boomtown.

By 1881, Joe Goldwater also had moved to Tombstone, where he hoped to make a comeback. In palmier days, he had shipped merchandise to Tombstone and made a loan to an acquaintance, P.W. Smith, who was starting a store in the new mining camp. Now it was time to collect. With son Lemuel in tow, Joe arrived as the town was recovering from a devastating fire that had wiped out much of the business district. Despite Tombstone's charred and raw appearance, he liked what he saw. Business was on the rebound, and Smith's losses in the fire had not been as severe as expected. He began paying Goldwater back. Soon Joe had resources sufficient to go into the general merchandise business for himself.

As Tombstone's prosperity and infamy reached its peak early in the 1880s, Tucson businesses opened branches there. Furniture dealer Leo Goldschmidt operated a Tombstone outlet, as did William Zeckendorf. Managed by Sol Schwab, it advertised as featuring the latest in goods imported from the East and Europe. William's competitor and brother Louis set up a general store in the nearby ore-processing center, Charleston, a town said to be even more raucous than Tombstone. The store was under the management of Sam Katzenstein, related by marriage to the Drachman brothers, and Albert Steinfeld. Louis would later sell the store to Sam.

Jews operated a variety of independent specialty stores. B. Laventhal and Rudolph Cohen transformed their general stores into men's clothing and furnishing shops. Emil Marks was a barber, and Philip Gotthelf sold tobacco products. The tailoring houses of J. Meyer & Brother and Samuel Black, L. Cohen's One Price Lace Store and M. Rosendorf's City of Paris Dry Goods Store, which offered ladies' fashions displayed in "show windows draped in San Francisco style," kept Tombstone's residents well dressed. In 1882, the City of Paris was purchased by brothers William, Simon and Louis Goldbaum, merchants from San Diego, who sold out the stock of ladies' goods and transformed the business into a men's clothing store. Sol Israel saw to the town's literary requirements at his bookstore and circulating library.

BANKING COMES TO TOMBSTONE

During Tombstone's heyday, the volume of business transacted, both mining and commercial, attracted the interest of the Jacobs brothers of Tucson. While they did not see a merchandising opportunity, they concluded that a bank would be profitable. Over the summer of 1880, therefore, Lionel

The Jacobs brothers brought banking to Tombstone with their Pima County Bank branch. Customers included Virgil Earp, John Slaughter and a Mr. Seligman. *Courtesy John Langellier, Tucson, Arizona.*

and Barron opened a branch of their Pima County Bank. For a while, they employed Hyman Solomon, recently arrived from San Diego and manager of the wholesale merchandise and liquor firm of Oberfelder & Company, as cashier. By the following summer, however, Solomon had become the general manager of the Tombstone agency. When the Pima County Bank became the First National Bank of Tucson a year later, the Tombstone branch ceased to exist since the National Banking Act prohibited territorial banks from operating branches. Barron and Lionel then incorporated a nominally independent Cochise County Bank under the laws of the territory. In 1882, the citizens of Tombstone elected Solomon city treasurer by a large majority. He also continued as manager of the Cochise County Bank until the Tombstone mines began to falter. Solomon left town in 1883, and Lionel Jacobs took over as president and general manager until the mines finally played out and the bank closed seven years later.

Abraham Emanuel, Mine Boss and Mayor

Abraham Hyman Emanuel arrived in Tombstone in 1880. For the next thirty years, he would be a major figure in the politics and economy of Cochise County. Abraham was born around 1838 into a well-to-do Philadelphia family. He became foreman at the Gould and Curry and the Yellow Jacket Mining Companies in Virginia City, Nevada, where he also operated a livery stable and freighting business. When he received word of the strike

Mining entrepreneur and Tombstone mayor Abraham Hyman Emanuel. *Courtesy Arizona State Library, Archives and Public Records, History and Archives Division, #97-9623, Phoenix.*

at Tombstone, Abraham packed up and moved to southern Arizona. There he worked as superintendent of Tombstone's Waterville Mill and Mining Company, the Tombstone Water Mill and Lumber Company and the Vizina Consolidated Mine. He later sold claims at the Vizina to Virgil and Wyatt Earp. Abraham also continued his livery business and branched out into freight wagon construction. With a luxuriant dark moustache and sharp eyes and sporting a two-carat diamond stickpin, he was a distinctive figure on the streets of Tombstone. It was said that he looked like a character right out of a Bret Harte story.

During Tombstone's long decline, Abraham remained active in mining. He was considered one of the most knowledgeable mining men in the district, even though politics began taking more and more of his time. In 1889, he was appointed clerk of the Cochise County Court, and in 1896, Tombstone voters elected him mayor. He won two more terms before losing the 1902 election. Following this loss, he moved to Tucson and eventually Los Angeles, where he died in March 1915. Over his lifetime, Abraham made, lost and remade fortunes, but he never married and left no survivors.

"Black Jack" Newman Had a Nose for Ore

The source of Black Jack's name is obscure. He probably picked up Newman during the time he spent laboring for the Texas and Pacific Railroad or in the mines of Globe, Arizona. In any case, he was the "new man" on the crew. He became Newman. The "Black Jack" nickname is a bit more difficult to ascertain. Perhaps the grime on his face when he worked in a Pennsylvania coal mine led to the moniker. Alternately, his skill with cards, particularly playing blackjack, may have caused folks to associate him with that game.

Born in 1862 in the Austro-Hungarian Empire, the young Jewish lad ran away from home at age fourteen and managed to work his way to America. He arrived in Arizona in the early 1880s, but because he was almost illiterate, his job opportunities were limited. He found employment as a mucker (worker who removes broken rock and waste from a mine) at Globe's Old Dominion Mine. Especially frugal, Newman saved enough money to begin working the Pioneer Mine, which was supposedly played out. Somehow, Newman knew different, and within a short time he and a partner had made $330,000 from the Pioneer. His partner, however, was not content and began stealing from the partnership. The two men fought. When the partner drew

John "Black Jack" Newman had a talent for finding rich silver and copper deposits. His discoveries helped establish the Miami mining district. *Courtesy Arizona Jewish Historical Society, Phoenix, Arizona.*

a knife, Newman pulled his .45 revolver and shot him in the arm, causing him to lose the limb. Although most observers thought it was a case of self-defense, at trial in 1889, the court sentenced Newman to ten years at Yuma. Evidently, the mining man had friends in high places, because the governor pardoned him after just one year.

Newman returned to the Globe area and resumed developing mines. He took some time off to enlist in the First Territorial Infantry during the Spanish-American War. Newman and his regiment, however, never got closer to Cuba than a camp in Georgia. Following his mustering out, Newman's success in mining continued. He seemed so lucky that many miners felt he had a nose for ore. It was as though he could just walk over ground and mysteriously know if there were rich diggings beneath. In addition to opening up mines, Newman acquired substantial tracts of real estate in the Globe/Miami area and constructed several buildings, including apartment houses, offices and two hotels, the Dominion and the Pioneer. Locals quoted him as saying about the hotels: "Vell, how you going to sell anything to these big mining investors unless you give 'em somewhere to stay and something to eat. Ve neffer get dem into town unless we treat 'em right, ain't it?"

Newman did sell his holdings to the big mining interests, including the Lewisohn family who established the Miami Copper Company. By the early twentieth century, Newman had become a millionaire, allowing him to purchase land in Arizona, Southern California, the San Joaquin valley, Texas and Arkansas. He retired to the West Coast and with his non-Jewish family settled into one of the largest homes in Santa Monica. He died of complications following surgery in April 1928.

THE WANDERING JEW

They called him "Lucky Mark" Lulley, and this son of Hungarian Jews was just that. He sought and made his fortune by scouring the mountains of southern Arizona and burrowing repeatedly into the earth in search of a big bonanza.

Born in Washington, D.C., in 1859, Mark arrived in Arizona at age eighteen in the company of his brother, Louis. They had been drawn by news of rich silver strikes in southern Arizona and initially settled in Tucson, where they tried their hand at storekeeping and running a saloon, without much success. The brothers found their way to Nogales, where, once again, they entered the dry goods and saloon businesses. Bored with these occupations, Mark decided to become a prospector. He outfitted with tortillas, hardtack, a pick, shovel and pan, a rifle and a burro. Mark assumed the nickname the "Wandering Jew" and set out for the hills and canyons north of town. At first, all he found was dirt and rock, but finally he staked a number of minor claims, which he sold. Mark's big strike came when he expanded his search to the Santa Rita Mountains and discovered a pocket of rich silver ore. He named his find, appropriately, the Wandering Jew. Elated with the discovery, he could not wait to tell his brother. Louis took an interest in the mine and probably provided the financial backing for its development.

The Wandering Jew mine prospered through the turn of the twentieth century. At its height, it consisted of two shafts, each about one hundred feet deep. From these extended a number of tunnels and crosscuts, making a total of about two thousand linear feet of subsurface mining development. Workers and their families lived in a small settlement that became known as the Jew Camp. Over this miniature empire, the brothers reigned supreme as mine owners and operators, civil authorities, principal merchants and most prominent residents. With the proceeds from the mine, Mark staked and developed other claims, but it would always be the Wandering Jew with which he would be most associated. Over time, however, the ore declined in quality and quantity and the Jew Camp's population dwindled until it was just another ghost town. But that did not keep Mark from self-promoting as a consultant on the mineral wealth of southern Arizona.

Louis and Mark remained prominent in the Nogales area, operating the Monte Carlo Club Room; newspaper advertisements proclaimed: "All games on the square." Louis also started Lulley's Buffet and catering business and opened the Casino Bar. Located along the international line, this establishment prided itself on being the "finest Sporting Resort in Nogales." It offered, in addition to the usual drinking and gambling attractions, free entertainment nightly by, "high class artists." Lucky Mark also returned to saloon keeping and merchandising in his later years.

Besides mining and business interests, Mark Lulley liked to hike and explore. While on one such expedition in the Santa Rita Mountains during the summer of 1900, he came upon a couple of seemingly abandoned bear cubs. After looking about for an upset mama bear, he determined the cubs were orphaned and brought them back to Nogales. The pair became objects of curiosity and amusement in the border city, but everyone knew that eventually the cubs would mature into not-so-cute bears without the skills to survive in the wild. Fortunately, the presidential contest between Republican William McKinley and Democrat William Jennings Bryan offered a solution. A staunch Democrat, Mark became involved in a wager on the election's outcome. If Bryan lost, he would take the bears to Washington, D.C., where they would participate in the inaugural parade and then be donated to the Smithsonian Institution's zoo. McKinley won, and on February 9, 1901, Mark and the bears boarded a train to his old hometown. After walking down Pennsylvania Avenue with his four-legged companions and being received at the White House, Mark bade them a fond farewell at the zoo gates.

Both Mark and Louis married Mexican women. Staunch Catholics, Mark's in-laws were so upset that their daughter had wed a Jew that they disowned her. How the family of Louis's wife felt about their daughter marrying a Jew is not known. Mark died in 1916, and his brother arranged for his body to be shipped to the District of Columbia and interred at the Washington Hebrew Congregation Cemetery. Louis passed away in 1928. His modest, cracked tombstone can be found in the City of Nogales Cemetery.

The Ezekiels of Ezekielsville

While not as active (or successful) as the Lulleys, brothers Alexander, Marcus "Mark" and Louis Ezekiels also prospected along the border during the late nineteenth century. Dutch Jews, the family lived in London prior to migrating to New York, where Mark and Louis were born. The 1880 census for Arizona listed Louis as a prospector in Pima County. His movements prior to that are sketchy, but Mark had been living in San Francisco. Mark's first job in the territory came in 1881 as a clerk at a store in Galeyville, a mining and smelter town and outlaw hangout in the far southeast. From there, both brothers roamed the mountains to the south and west looking for mineral wealth, but with limited success. In 1882, the camp of Ezekielsville came into existence at a silver mine near the ruins of old Forts Buchanan and Crittenden. Like the mine itself, the camp was pretty ephemeral, with building materials consisting of canvas, blankets, brush and whatever the inhabitants could scrounge from the deteriorating army posts. As with most mining camps, Ezekielsville had its share of violence, including an incident in 1882 which saw Mark shoot a cowboy who assaulted him and attempted to steal a horse. He wounded the miscreant in the arm and turned him over to the sheriff.

Ezekielsville did not last long, but that did not deter the brothers from continuing to look for the elusive strike. That came in 1899 when Louis discovered the Cuprite copper mine in the Santa Rita Mountains southeast of Tucson. The Cuprite was never a major producer, but Louis worked it for a while and then leased it to provide an income. He went on to manage other mines in the region and operate a sawmill. Louis remained in southern Arizona, taking up law enforcement and serving on posses that chased outlaws, including the Apache Kid. He later worked as a detective and fingerprint expert for the Tucson Police Department. Louis died in 1931. Alexander took up mining near Mammoth, Arizona, and went into police work as a U.S. marshal. Mark married Valencia Lulley and eventually moved to Montana. Prior to leaving Arizona, their daughter, Rebecca, married Charles Carr Clark, an army officer stationed at Tucson. Their son, Mark Clark, became a noted general in World War II.

Henry Lesinsky, Arizona's Copper Baron

Henry Lesinsky knew mining. Born in German Poland, teenaged Henry had been sent by his father to England to learn stone and wood carving. From there he immigrated to Australia, where he worked in the gold mines, and then to the California Mother Lode, where he increased his knowledge of mining techniques. By the late 1860s, he had joined his uncle Julius Freudenthal in New Mexico. Henry kept abreast of mining activities in Arizona. After a try at storekeeping in Tucson, Lesinsky and five heavily armed men braved the very real dangers of Apache ambush to stake out seven claims in eastern Arizona. In return for $10,000 paid to Robert and James Metcalf, the original locators, he and his uncle Julius obtained a majority interest. They set about gathering the equipment and skilled labor to begin operations. Henry also brought his brother Charles and a Silver City, New Mexico business associate, David Abraham, into the partnership. Within a year, their mines were in production, although production did not always mean profits.

The village that grew up along the San Francisco River near the mines came to be known as Clifton. It first consisted of adobe huts that housed workers, superintendents and owners. The largest structure in the community was the company store. For some time, this was the only profit making aspect of Lesinsky's venture. This lack of quick returns disillusioned the Metcalfs, who sold out their remaining interest to Lesinsky in 1874. Lesinsky later stated he paid the Metcalfs $20,000, but Robert Metcalf claimed he had been cheated and threatened to kill him. Lesinsky paid no attention and reorganized the operation into the Longfellow Copper Company with himself as chief officer; Charles as vice president; and Julius Freudenthal, who had moved to New York, as the firm's treasurer and eastern agent. Lesinsky, nevertheless, had trouble making a go of this copper mine.

Copper magnate Henry Lesinsky, developer of the Clifton-Morenci mines. *Courtesy Arizona Jewish Historical Society, Phoenix, Arizona.*

Initially, the most pressing problem facing Lesinsky was isolation. Silver City, the nearest settlement of any consequence, was some eighty miles to the southeast. Machinery and supplies had to be hauled in and copper ore shipped out by large freight wagons over virtually nonexistent roads. The wagon trains to Silver City did so under the constant threat of Apache ambush until well into the 1880s. Moving tons of ore by slow wagons from the mines to the processing works at Clifton also hampered copper production. In 1879, Lesinsky finally replaced the mule-drawn wagons with the more efficient Coronado Railroad, a twenty-inch "Baby Gauge" line between the mines and mill.

The smelter also proved to be a challenge. In the early years, copper ore had to be freighted to smelters in the east. This arrangement proved costly and time-consuming. To solve this problem, Lesinsky elected to build his own smelting works at Clifton. As early as the autumn of 1873, he constructed a Mexican-style furnace for smelting ore. Fires from wood gathered locally were not hot enough to accomplish the task, so Lesinsky contracted Isadore Solomon to supply high grade charcoal. The extreme heat, while adequate for smelting ore, often caused the adobe furnace to collapse. He tried stone and fired brick, but after each attempt, all that remained was a pile of warm rubble. The company's production and profits stagnated until 1876, when, after another unsuccessful test, Lesinsky noticed that a piece of copper used to plug a hole in the smelter wall had held, where adobe, brick and stone had failed. Lesinsky ordered construction of a new copper-lined smelter and began producing an average of seventy-five thousand pounds of copper per month.

Now that he was turning out copper, Lesinsky had to deal with depressed markets. He reduced expenses whenever and wherever possible. Some of these tactics caused grumbling among his workers. He hired miners and smelter men at a promised wage level but later paid them in Mexican currency, which had a lesser value than American dollars. Workers also received scrip redeemable only at the company store, managed by his nephew Samuel Freudenthal. The company saloon allegedly watered down its drinks to cut costs. As a last-ditch effort, Lesinsky imported Chinese laborers from California, a move that aroused the anger of white workers. "Let it be remembered as a matter of Arizona history," a journalist wrote acidly, "that the first importation of Chinese cheap slave labor…was made by one H. Lesinsky."

Although Lesinsky's economy measures may have been unpopular, they did keep the Clifton mines afloat, and by the late 1870s, he was receiving attractive offers for the property. But rather than accept the first bid, he decided to take his family on a yearlong grand tour of Europe in 1880. Upon his return, he found that the value of his mines and smelter had increased dramatically. The invention of the telephone and other electrically driven devices had driven up the demand for copper. In addition, construction of the Southern Pacific Railroad across southern Arizona and New Mexico put Clifton much nearer a rail connection. By 1882, Lesinsky no longer had the inclination to carry on the Clifton operation. For ten years, he and his family had endured the hardships of frontier life. Lesinsky concluded that he had earned whatever profit that he could make from the sale. When the deal concluded, a syndicate of Scottish capitalists paid him and his company $1,250,000 for the mines, railroad and smelter. A jubilant Lesinsky wrote, "Here was a change of affairs. Ten years of agony were forgotten….We had reached the promised land at last." He died in 1924 a wealthy man.

Jake Abraham Clifton's Hotelier, Par Excellence

The development of the Clifton mines by Henry Lesinsky attracted a number of Jewish businessmen—storekeepers, tailors, jewelers, grocers and professionals. One of the most noted among these was Jake Abraham, Clifton's hotelier. He boasted the finest lodging house in the region, with a "New Building, Well Ventilated Rooms, Eastern Furniture." Rates began at fifty cents a night. An early account written by a guest, however, indicated that these claims stretched the truth to the breaking point. One portion of the hotel was reserved for guests behind in their bills:

> *It was built of undressed 1-inch lumber and surmounted by a canvas roof. Each room was divided from its neighbor by sheets of cheese-cloth nailed to scantlings, and the ceiling was conspicuous by its absence. It had mysterious powers akin to what is now known as wireless. A whisper at one end of the row could be easily heard at the other; and that is how it came to be known as Telephone Row. In summer time it acted as a Turkish bath during the day, and in winter it filled the role of a refrigerator during the night, and it was to the local scorpions and tarantulas what the Riviera is to the Parisian. They could not keep away from it. On Sundays, Jake gave us wine to dinner, and what a wine it was! Shipped in barrels from California, it had the consistency of crude oil and the soporific quality of chloroform. After a hearty meal sluiced down with this ambrosial nectar, the thirty odd boarders walked to their seats under the verandah, and there promptly fell asleep.*

Jake's hotel served the Clifton community well and provided lodging for mining investors, speculators, geologists and engineers. Jake eventually gave up the hotel, which his wife ran for a while, but returned to it after the turn of the twentieth century with his brother Sam as proprietor and Jake as manager.

Kings of the Copper Queen

Henry Lesinsky and his family left Arizona for New York soon after the sale of the Clifton properties, but Jewish involvement in copper mining did not end with their departure. When the discoverers of the Copper Queen mine near the Mexican border brought rich ore samples to Louis Zeckendorf's

Tucson store, the merchant quickly obtained an option on the property. He promoted it to a group of San Francisco investors, who put between $16,000 and $20,000 into the Copper Queen and adjoining Copper King claims. Zeckendorf became secretary/treasurer of this syndicate, which soon constructed a smelter and began production. He also built a wagon road from the mines to the Southern Pacific Railroad at Benson and furnished the wagons to haul the copper bullion.

Louis figured he could make money from the Copper Queen in a number of ways—from the ore itself, from freighting equipment and supplies to the mine and ore from it, from a store serving the miners and by encouraging other businessmen to invest. The discovery of a new rich body of ore led to a legal conflict with the neighboring Atlanta Mine, which was controlled by the New York–based Phelps Dodge Company. Rather than face a lengthy and expensive court fight, Zeckendorf negotiated a merger with Phelps Dodge, which took over operations in 1882.

An Old Boot Ends a Partnership

From the 1870s through the 1890s, Zeckendorf also became interested in mines in Pinal County near the confluence of the Gila River and Mineral Creek southeast of Phoenix. He acquired the faltering Pinal Copper Company and its claims at the mining community of Ray in 1883. Along with Albert Steinfeld, Zeckendorf put together a new firm called the Ray Copper Company. Zeckendorf served as secretary/treasurer, while Steinfeld managed the mining and smelting works as well as the company store. Zeckendorf and Steinfeld operated the Ray mines until 1889, when they sold them to an English concern.

Zeckendorf and Steinfeld also acquired copper mines at Silverbell (about forty miles northwest of Tucson). Disputes that arose during the sale of the Ray properties and a convoluted argument over the Old Boot Mine at Silverbell caused profound changes not only in their mining interests but in their commercial and personal relationships as well. Actually, Louis had for some time disapproved of Steinfeld's management of the mines and stores. A visit by Louis to Tucson in 1901 did nothing to resolve the differences. If anything, it made the situation worse, and within a year Louis was considering selling his interest in the company. Legal and personal wrangling continued for another couple of years, until February 1904, when Louis sued for dissolution of L. Zeckendorf and Company claiming mismanagement by his nephew. The issue was resolved in May with the unhappy termination of the family partnership. Even though the firm had been dissolved, the two men continued to battle it out all the way to the U.S. Supreme Court. The struggle lasted until 1915, when Louis finally prevailed. By that time, however, Albert was established as southern Arizona's leading merchant and the decision had little effect on his business.

SMELTER TOWN...THE JEWS OF DOUGLAS

In 1902, the Calumet and Arizona Company built a copper smelter along the Mexican border near the U.S. Army's Camp San Bernardino in southeastern Arizona. Two years later, the Phelps Dodge Company blew in a second smelter. The town of Douglas grew up in the barren desert around the smelters. A number of Jews settled in the new community as workers for the mining companies, storekeepers and tailors serving military units stationed along the border. The most prosperous of these merchants were the Levys. In February 1903, Jacob Levy and his wife, Mamie, opened

Interior of Jacob Levy's Red Star Store in Douglas around the turn of the century. The Levys later relocated to Tucson and founded what became a major department store. *Author's collection.*

what they called the Red Star General Store in Douglas. Jacob, the son of Lithuanian and German immigrants, had come to Arizona from Texas, where he operated a small general store. The new business prospered, and eventually a second story was added. Jacob's brother Ben, who had been foreman of a "bull gang" building a railroad line from Cananea, Sonora, to Douglas, also joined the firm. The Levys eventually moved their main shop to Tucson, where it would become one of the city's leading department stores.

The Jewish community of Douglas was close-knit, and in 1904 it established a cemetery. By 1907, the smelter town could boast a Jewish population of about ninety men and women who had formed a congregation called the Sons of Israel and met regularly for services and holidays. Jews would remain a vital part of Douglas's business and social life well into the twentieth century.

7

WILD AND DANGEROUS DAYS

Cowboys and Indians, bad men and lawmen, showdowns and gunfights—nineteenth-century Arizona was thought of as the wildest territory in the West. Jews who came to Arizona, particularly during the early years, quickly encountered these unstable surroundings. If they did not know already, they learned how to handle firearms and defend themselves. They avoided ambushes and interacted as peaceably as possible with neighbors who might not be living on the right side of the law or who fought to hold on to their traditional lands. Those who could not adapt usually left on the next stagecoach or train for a more settled and peaceful home.

Jim Levy, a Hard Man...But Was He Jewish?

In the Old West, few occupations were as colorful or controversial as a gunfighter. Town bully or hired assassin, a gunfighter almost always had a nasty reputation. But a Jewish shootist named Levy? Yup—at least some folks think so. The question remains, however, was legendary gunslinger Jim Levy really Jewish? His origins in Ireland might give pause to those claiming his Jewish heritage. Added to this is the spelling of his name on some official documents as Leavey, which would be unusual for a Jew. Nevertheless, many writers stick with his name as Levy and his Jewishness. But Jew or Gentile, as a child, Jim Levy came to the United States with his parents. He pursued a violent path through Nevada, Wyoming, North Dakota and, finally, Arizona.

Gunslinger Jim Levy (or Leavey) met his end by ambush on the dusty street in front of Tucson's Palace Hotel. *Courtesy Arizona Historical Society, #18762, Tucson, Arizona.*

Along the way, Levy worked as a gambler and gunman, gaining a reputation as a cool *pistolero* and the respect of Wyatt Earp and Bat Masterson. He was said to rely on a steady hand rather than a quick draw, although he could slip leather fast enough when the need arose. According to his legend, Levy engaged in over sixteen gunfights.

Levy resided in Tombstone during the silver boom, plying his trade as a gambler, but by June 1882 he had made his way to Tucson. There he and a faro dealer got into an altercation and agreed to shoot it out at the international line. His opponent, however had a different plan. Realizing that he likely would not survive a duel with Levy, he and a couple of sidekicks ambushed the gunfighter in front of Tucson's Palace Hotel. The possibly Irish Jew fell dead. His best epitaph was pronounced by one of his assassins: "Levy was a hard man."

Ambushes on the Trail

The trails from the Colorado River to the mining districts of central Arizona in the 1860s and 1870s could be treacherous. Narrow, rocky and rutted in the summer, boggy and sometimes snowy in winter, these roads also were favorite haunts of the Yavapai and Apache and offered ample locations for ambushes. Attacks on travelers, pack trains and freight wagons were not uncommon. In one such incident, Michael Wormser was accompanying one of his mule trains to Prescott when Indians ambushed it and the portly merchant suffered the indignity of either an arrow or bullet wound to his ample posterior. While the injury did not prove serious, it was embarrassing and did little to improve Wormser's already sour disposition.

The brothers Goldwater along with their longtime friend and partner Dr. Wilson W. Jones also found the trip from Prescott to be dangerous. In June 1872, they were ambushed by Indians while traveling from Fort Whipple to Ehrenberg. Although Mike and Dr. Jones in the lead buggy had their clothes perforated, they made it through otherwise unscathed. Joe, trailing in another buggy, took bullets in the back and shoulder. Amid clouds of dust, gun smoke and flying lead, the travelers, even the wounded Joe, raced ahead in what seemed to be a futile attempt to outrun their pursuers. Finally, a party of ranchers happened upon the scene and drove off the attackers. Dr. Jones treated Joe's painful wounds as best he could, and the unfortunate merchant later received care from an army surgeon. Joe's injuries, however, were serious enough to cause him to return to San Francisco for an extended recuperation. From then on, Mike did not venture on the trail without a rifle.

On June 4, 1870, a group of Tucsonans was attacked by the Apaches on a road outside of town. Listed among the dead was a Newton Israel, former store owner at Camp Grant and now a well-known rancher. When they gathered enough courage to return to the scene of the fight, the survivors found poor Israel scalped and burned alive.

Travel farther into the interior of the territory could be even more hazardous. One story has it that while pursuing the salt trade in the 1860s, Sol Barth and his workers were taken prisoner by a band of Chiricahua Apaches, possibly led by Cochise. He and his companions kept their freedom, and their scalps, however, when another chief, friendly with Barth, interceded on their behalf. Nevertheless, they were robbed of all their possessions and forced to strip naked before being expelled from camp to walk to the nearest settlement. On other occasions, along with partner Aaron Barnett, Barth risked ambush and robbery while carrying the mail between Prescott and Albuquerque and Prescott and Tucson on government contracts. They often traveled at night and rested during the day to avoid trouble with Indians. Some of their employees were not so fortunate. At least two mail riders met their deaths on the route.

Shot in the Back

No one could deny that Heyman Mannasse was an unpleasant man. A notorious womanizer who had deserted his wife in California to come to Arizona, he did not get along with many people, but he was a good businessman with a reputation for honesty. Heyman operated stores in Phoenix and Wickenburg. It was in Wickenburg that he met a violent end.

It happened on the morning of April 20, 1875. Heyman got into an argument with a freighter named Jesus Amado over the price for hauling barley to Ehrenberg. As the dispute became more heated, Amado refused to transport the barley or any other freight. Heyman accused him of lying and reneging on their deal. When the freighter hit Heyman in the face, he pulled out his revolver and fired twice at Amado but missed. Amado then went to his wagon to get his own firearm. As he headed back to the store to shoot it out, he saw Heyman loading a shotgun. Rather than waiting for his opponent to finish, Amado shot him in the back. Heyman did not survive. Amado beat a hasty retreat to the Colorado, where he caught a boat downriver and disappeared into Mexico. When Heyman's brother, Moses, settled the estate, he found it to be in excess of $12,000 (or over $270,000 in today's money). No one ever said that Heyman Mannasse was not a good businessman.

King of the Outlaws Meets a Schuster Shotgun

May 30, 1888, started out as a slow day at the A. and B. Schuster store in Holbrook. Adolf puttered around the merchandise until a red-headed

The Schuster Brothers original Holbrook store. "Red" McNeil held up the brothers here, getting away with some cash and a little buckshot. *Courtesy A&B Schuster Collection, Museum of Northern Arizona, Flagstaff, Arizona.*

customer came in. He asked for an item, and as Adolf reached for it, pulled a revolver and ordered the storekeeper to open the safe. Adolf complied, but as the robber started to leave with about $200, he ran up against Ben, who carried a shotgun. Since Adolf stood between them, Ben could not fire right away. The two did exchange gunfire, as the bad man fled with a few pellets of buckshot in his back, but no one was seriously hurt. The Schusters thought the robber bore a striking resemblance to W.R. "Red" McNeil, a cowboy with the Hashknife outfit who had a bad reputation around Holbrook. A posse set out after McNeil. They did not catch him, but they did find a poem he had attached to a tree. In the first stanza, the robber-poet boasted:

> *I am king of the outlaws / I am perfection at robbing a store…*

And he went on to taunt his most recent victims:

> *They are my kind friends, the Schusters / For whom I carry so much lead*
> *In the future to kill this young rooster / They will have to aim at his head.*

The law never caught up with McNeil, at least for this crime, but decades later, the robber, who seemed to have reformed himself, paid Adolf a couple of visits. They reminisced about times gone by in Holbrook, although Schuster could not quite recall how he knew the familiar gentleman. On the second visit, Red let the retired merchant know who he was, but once again the two old-timers enjoyed each other's company and tales of the past, Adolf having long since forgiven Arizona's "Pistol Packing Poet."

THE BISBEE MASSACRE

While Red McNeil's assault on A. and B. Schuster in Holbrook did not result in any deaths or even serious injuries, the robbery of Joe Goldwater's Bisbee store was a different matter. The development of the Copper Queen mine in the early 1880s led to the establishment of the mining camp of Bisbee east of Nogales and just north of the Mexican border. Fortune seekers flocked to the new settlement, its main streets perched precariously along Tombstone Canyon and Brewery Gulch. One of the earliest storekeepers was the peripatetic Joe Goldwater. After the difficulty in Yuma, he had wandered about the territory, going to Prescott for a visit with Michael and Morris and then to Phoenix. Both locations, however, did not offer any business opportunities. So, it was on to the silver boomtown of Tombstone.

After a while in Tombstone, Joe once again got itchy feet. Within a few months, he had sold out and relocated to Contention, a mill site for the Tombstone mines on the San Pedro River. He also opened stores in nearby Fairbank and at Benson on the Southern Pacific mainline. Along the way, he picked up a couple of partners—Joseph Guindani and Jose Miguel Castaneda. Their firm, called A.A. Castaneda, took its name from Jose Miguel's wife, Amparo Arvisu, since all three men had been bankrupts and could not easily get credit. They opened a general store in Bisbee, which prospered from the start.

Joe's great-nephew Barry Goldwater related the story that by late 1883, the Goldwater-Castaneda store had become a sort of bank for the surrounding vicinity. Miners cashed their paychecks and kept valuables in the safe. More importantly, the safe had become the depository for the Copper Queen's monthly payroll, usually several thousand dollars. This, in particular, attracted the attention of a gang of robbers. On the evening of December 3, 1883, they rode into town and stopped in front

Bisbee's dusty main street about the time of the infamous massacre. *Courtesy Arizona State Library, Archives and Public Records, History and Archives Division, #96-3296, Phoenix.*

of the Goldwater-Castaneda store. Joe likely did not pay much attention as they dismounted and walked in. They covered their faces with kerchiefs and pulled out Winchesters and pistols. Inside the store were Joe; his son Lemuel, who was helping a customer; bookkeeper Peter Doll; and Castaneda, who was ill in bed in the back. The robbers demanded the safe be opened, but when Lemuel and Doll protested that they did not know the combination, the gang became agitated and moved on to Joe. They ordered Joe to put up his hands, prompting the wily storekeeper to engage in a bit of banter, stalling for time and hoping the law would arrive soon: "You come in here and say 'hands up' and my hands go up. Then you say 'open the safe.' I am no magician. Tell me how to do it." The robbers replied that they would blow Joe's brains out if he did not comply, to which Joe responded, "Who then will open the safe? What will you gain by that?" A demand for the mine payroll followed, and Joe played his trump card: "That is where you get fooled. The stagecoach is late. The payroll is not here."

His assailants failed to see the irony in Joe's remark and leveled their weapons at him, at which point the merchant figured that further conversation would likely get him killed and opened the safe. Inside were the store's receipts, somewhere in the neighborhood of $600 to $900. Joe was right. The payroll had not yet arrived. They then had Joe empty the contents of the safe into a sack and proceeded to relieve the staff and customers of their valuables. By that time, gunfire could be heard in front of the building. In the fracas that followed, the gang shot down anyone who appeared on the street. In all, four citizens died that day, including a lawman and a pregnant woman, earning the incident the name "Bisbee Massacre." As the robbers finally exited to make their getaway, Joe was said to have called after them: "It will be a cold night. Maybe you'd better take some blankets."

Joe was lucky that his impertinence did not result in a bullet heading in his direction. Once the shooting stopped, an enraged citizenry mounted two posses, but the leader of one group turned out to be the robber who had put the gang up to the robbery in the first place. Needless to say, his confederates got away, at least for a while. Eventually, legitimate lawmen brought the outlaws to justice, including the mastermind. Five were tried and hanged. The sixth, the ringleader who had misled the posse, escaped with a life sentence but later was taken from the Tombstone jail by a mob and lynched.

Joe's coolness in a bad situation that day made him somewhat of a celebrity in Bisbee. His bravado may have been genuine or prompted by nervousness. He later remarked that his main objective was to get the outlaws out of his store as quickly as possible. Pretty soon it was back to storekeeping for Joe Goldwater, but there were still trials ahead. A fire in February 1885 caused considerable damage to the Bisbee store. Joe's health also began to decline. Diagnosed with malaria, he spent less and less time at the store and more time resting at a local hotel, where Jose Castaneda's mother-in-law cared for him. The two married in San Francisco in October 1887, but their life together was short. They returned to Bisbee where, on August 31, 1889, Joseph Goldwater died at the age of fifty-five. It would be up to Lemuel to close operations in southern Arizona. He then moved to Southern California, bringing to an end the Goldwater presence along the border.

A Holdup Foiled

Isadore Elkhan Solomon traveled a lot by stagecoach in the Gila River valley. The conveyances were uncomfortable and susceptible to robbery. Such was the case when a gang stopped the coach in which Solomon and some other passengers were riding. According to Solomon family lore, the holdup men told the driver and passengers to get down on the road and relieved them of their money and valuables. At that point, Solomon graciously thanked the robbers for not harming anyone. The miscreants seemed pleased with this remark, which Solomon followed up with a request for return of his watch. He said that this was a precious family heirloom. Touched by the explanation, the robbers gave back the watch. The other victims caught on to Solomon's gambit and did the same thing, one of them even offering to send the robbers one hundred dollars by mail. The bandits declined, saying that they did not need a reward, and returned the passengers' valuables. Solomon then asked for some money so that they could buy food and drink. He must have had quite a presence, since the robbers again acquiesced and gave him a bit of the loot. With that, the brigands realized that the negotiations were not going their way. They mounted their horses and galloped off with a take considerably less than originally anticipated.

Stagecoach in Prescott. Isadore Solomon rode in a similar vehicle when he and his traveling companions were held up. *Courtesy Arizona State Library, Archives and Public Records, History and Archives Division, #98-072, Phoenix.*

"You Can Hang a Jew"

In 1872, Vicente Hernandez and Librada Chavez moved to Tucson from New Mexico. The young couple wanted to open a store and went to see a merchant known to help tendejones, William Zeckendorf. William had a reputation for frequently backing small merchants, mostly ambitious Mejicanos like Vicente and Librada. With some money and a stock of merchandise provided by Zeckendorf, the two established a modest general store, the rear of which they turned into living quarters. Vicente and Librada proved to be a good investment. Hard workers, within a year they had repaid their debt and expanded the business to include pawnbroking. As his income increased, Vicente deposited his receipts in William's safe, and the two men became business associates, if not friends.

Two woodchoppers who worked nearby probably saw the number of customers that the store attracted. Surely, they reckoned, such a popular establishment must have quite a bit of cash in its till, and pawnbrokers always had money and valuables on hand. But neither had the nerve to act alone. So they brought in an acquaintance who quickly became the ringleader. On the night of August 5, they waited until the couple retired and all was quiet. Then the robbers made their move.

The next morning, a serving girl arrived to prepare breakfast and discovered a bloody crime scene. Vicente and Librada lay on the ground with their skulls bashed in and throats slit. The residence and store had been ransacked. A shaken Zeckendorf, accompanied by deputy sheriff Nathan Appel, rushed to the scene. William determined several items to be missing, including firearms and Vicente's silver watch. He also looked at the cash book and empty till. The robbers' take—thirty-seven dollars.

Soon the three not very careful robbers were in custody. The funeral of Vicente and Librada took place on the morning of Friday, August 8. Once the victims had been consigned to the earth, the crowd surged to the plaza in front of the courthouse. The sheriff, deputies, district attorney, judge and court staff made themselves scarce. In their place stood William, chair of the town's public safety committee. It was a moment made for the Irrepressible Z. The impresario of fireworks and fiestas climbed onto a wagon and in a solemn voice recounted the facts of the crime and evidence against the men. He also related the frequent inability of the court to render quick justice and the ease with which criminals got off on technicalities. William concluded his remarks by asking the assembled, "What punishment have the murderers deserved?" "Death!" came the resounding reply. A prominent Tucson Mejicano then addressed the crowd in Spanish and asked the same question. "*Que mueren*" (they must die), came the response. Satisfied that he had the citizenry behind him, William signaled for the condemned to be brought from the jail. Slowly they shuffled to the wagons placed below an improvised gallows, their legs still bound in chains to add weight to the death drop.

Then John Willis appeared. Willis was in jail on reprieve from a murder conviction. He had the misfortune to be in the wrong place at a very wrong time. William and the committee decided that rather than having this convicted murderer possibly escape justice there would be another noose on the plaza.

The condemned had black caps placed over their heads and nooses tightened around their necks. But just before the wagons on which they stood could be sent forward, a voice bellowed from the crowd, "You can hang a Mexican. You can hang a Jew. You can hang a n———. But you can't hang an American citizen!" The voice belonged to the former U.S. marshal for Arizona Milton Duffield, and he threatened violence should the execution of Willis proceed. The sixty-three-year-old Duffield was past his prime and clearly drunk but still could be a fearful opponent. He stood over six feet, three inches tall with a powerful build and a reputation for violence. But on this August morning, he misjudged the situation badly.

The crowd hushed. William glared over his spectacles. Not only had Duffield interrupted a perfectly orderly lynching, but he had cast aspersions on the merchant's Jewish heritage. Before William could come down and confront the ex-marshal, however, onlookers swarmed the tipsy giant, disarmed him and led him away. Committee members then drove the wagons from under the four men. A few convulsions and it was over.

But what of Duffield? His brief time in custody did not improve his mood a bit. He went after the four-eyed Jew storekeeper his pickled brain believed responsible for his troubles. He found the merchant and struck him with a club. Rather than going down, however, the Irrepressible Z turned and punched Duffield behind the ear, knocking him over. He then proceeded to pummel his assailant senseless. When he recovered, the ex-marshal went off to nurse his wounds, leaving William alone after that.

MARCUS GOLDBAUM...SCALPED!

Marcus Goldbaum was a man who took chances, and eventually this trait caught up with him. He and his family had come to the United States from Prussia in the 1850s and lived in Kansas, Colorado, California, Texas and New Mexico prior to arriving in Tucson in 1869. Marcus did not stay long in Tucson, however, moving on to Wickenburg, where he became a justice of the peace, then Florence, Benson, Harshaw, Tombstone and Phoenix. Finally, he returned to Tucson, where he worked as a butcher. With his wife, Sara, and their seven children, the Goldbaums became well known in Tucson's business and society. But dealing in meat was not Marcus's main interest. He was an inveterate prospector and took numerous gold hunting trips into the mountains. Eventually, he occupied a cabin in the Whetstone Mountains of Cochise County, turning over the butcher business to his wife. He should have stayed behind the meat counter. In 1886, while residing in his mining cabin, Marcus was killed by Apache raiders from Geronimo's band. Days later, a cavalry patrol found his body, or what was left of it. He appeared to have been taken by surprise, shot and scalped. Western artist Frederic Remington depicted the gory scene in

Jewish meat merchant and prospector Marcus Goldbaum met a grisly death at the hands of the Apaches. Artist Frederic Remington depicted the discovery of his body. *From John Bigelow,* On the Bloody Trail of Geronimo *(Los Angeles: Westernlore Press, 1958).*

a sketch published in the book *On the Bloody Trail of Geronimo*. Although they did not recognize him because of his wounds and decomposition, the soldiers buried Marcus. Later, his identity came to light. He was fifty-one years old at the time of his death.

Ironically, so the story goes, about the time that Marcus was meeting his end, his son Emilio, who followed in his father's footsteps as a prospector, rode out from Tucson to inspect a mine. He was himself ambushed by Apache warriors. They chased and shot at him for several miles. Emilio returned fire, but neither side scored any hits. Finally, Emilio found a safe haven at a stage station. Although Emilio Goldbaum made it unharmed back to the Old Pueblo, he did not let his brush with the Apaches deter his quest for riches. He continued searching for gold and silver in the mountains around Tucson but never forgot that a prospector's life could be dangerous, indeed.

Sam Aaron, "The Lucky Jew Kid"

Territorial Arizona could be a tough place for both Jew and Gentile. This was particularly true in the mining camps. Sam Aaron was one of those who met that challenge. Sam told his tales of life on the frontier to friends and acquaintances and eventually wrote them down. The first part of the manuscript told of Sam's life in the Arizona Territory, where he associated with miners, cowboys, gamblers, rustlers and stagecoach robbers. The document found its way into the American Jewish Archives in Cincinnati, Ohio, and was edited by Dr. Jacob Rader Marcus and published in 1958 in the journal *American Jewish Archives.* Whether everything in Sam's colorful narrative actually occurred—*Quién sabe?*

Sam Aaron was born in Salt Lake City in 1866 to a Jewish family that pioneered in Montana and California. His father, one of those restless Jewish merchants, sought opportunities wherever they might arise. He later moved the family to Galveston, New Orleans and New York. In 1877, Sam joined his father, who by then was in Butte City, Montana.

Sam should have had all the benefits of a good education, but beginning about age eleven he became infatuated with gambling and began frequenting the saloons where that pastime prevailed. He got an education alright, just not an academic one. Sam did have a career goal—faro dealer. When Tombstone boomed in the early 1880s, the Aarons were not far behind. His father had a general store there and was respected as one of the town's "honest" merchants. This reputation passed on to Sam, but instead of working inside the law, he held money for smugglers and rustlers until they could claim their ill-gotten gains.

Sam's father decided to have a store in Charleston and to do this became indebted to a Tucson liquor wholesaler named Max Oberfelder. Dad left Tucson for Charleston, giving Sam the money to pay the debt. But being a willful teenager, Sam had other ideas and lost the entire amount gambling. Panic set in. He got a job in the mill to earn back the loss. He was smart and advanced up the ranks of the operation, but gambling remained his passion. At that time, Charleston was a prime location for gamblers. Its population swelled on mine and mill paydays with workers eager to try to up their incomes. Sam became a faro dealer, and he was good at it, gaining the nickname, the "Lucky Jew Kid." Gambling could, at times, be a hazardous occupation. Sam tells of one such occasion:

> *Two Mexicans entered the saloon one night when the game was in progress. One of them made a bet of one dollar and turned his back to the game.*

In the meantime the dealer made a deal and the Mexican lost his dollar. The dealer made another deal and covered the other card. By that time the Mexican turned around and saw that his money was gone and, not having seen the operation, accused another player of taking his money. He started to raise a rough-house and called the dealer a s.o.b. in Mexican when I walked to him and tried to explain the transaction. But Mr. Mexican would not listen and wanted to fight. I immediately invited him out of the place. His partner had a forty-five caliber Smith & Wessen [sic] projecting from his holster. I hollered to my partner, who was in the back of the bar, to cover him. We had on the drain board of the bar a sawed-off shotgun, which Jack immediately picked up and covered the Mexican. As I got to the door this Mexican turned to fight, and I was fortunate enough to knock him out with one punch. I then took away from him a big knife. Jack put it among the collection of guns and knives.

A short while after, the Mexican gave a yell and I said to him in Spanish, "Keep quiet." He in turn said, "God damned fool." I took him to the door and he walked with me quietly; he threw his hand on the gun. I had no time to pull my gun, but put one hand on the open door and the other hand against the casing, lifted my foot and kicked him in the chin. He swung back to about forty-five degrees, held his balance, and leaned forward, and fell flat on his nose, bleeding heavily. I took the gun away, searched his person, left him to lie near his friend, and put his gun on the bar. He lay on the floor for about an hour, then came back into the saloon, approached and said to me, "Good boy" (in Mexican), pleading with me to give him back the knife and pistol, which request I denied.

For a while, Sam continued to work in the mill and at night ran the saloon in Charleston where he tended bar. The debt was repaid. He later helped lead millworkers in a successful strike at Charleston (which cost him his day job), became a deputy U.S. marshal and drove cattle. Eventually, Sam married a Catholic woman and wound up in Stockton, California, where he had a men's clothing store for a number of years. He died in Pomona, California, in September 1940. He received a Jewish funeral, but his widow later may have had his ashes reinterred in a Catholic cemetery.

Bulls and Bullets—Abe Franklin, His "Friend" Johnny Ringo

They called Abraham Maurice Franklin "Abe" or sometimes just the "Kid," and unlike his younger brother Selim, a successful Tucson attorney, legislator and civic leader, Abe spent much of his younger years in the saddle.

In 1877, the Jacobs brothers directed Abe to go to the head of the broad San Simon valley in the northeast corner of Cochise County near the almost ghost town of Galeyville. At the time, Galeyville was a favorite haunt of horse thieves and "cow wrestlers." They liked the place because of its seclusion from the prying eyes of lawmen and ranchers. Abe left reminiscences of one of his assignments to oversee one thousand head of cattle that had been on the hoof from Chihuahua and Durango, Mexico, and needed a rest before heading north. An old-time cowman by the name of Jim Sprague had charge of the herd. Abe knew that the leader of the rustlers was John Peters Ringo, better known as Johnny Ringo. Ringo had a reputation for violence, particularly against unarmed men, and as one of the best shots in the territory. He definitely could be trouble. But it would not be Ringo who first plagued the drovers, at least not directly. One night, after dinner and the first watch, something spooked the herd and it headed straight for Abe. He sensed the ground rumbling, jumped on his horse and took off, but the cattle continued gaining on him. It would not be long before he ended up trampled. At that point, one of the experienced cowboys yelled at him to circle about so that the cattle would follow him, stop running and settle down. The panicky cows must have thought Abe was leading the stampede because the maneuver worked, and the pandemonium subsided.

The next morning, scouts indicated that about 150 to 200 had run in the direction of Gayleyville and had been intercepted by a group of riders. Abe knew who that meant—Ringo. He also noticed that Sprague had disappeared and, putting two and two together, reasoned that his trail boss had been responsible for the stampede, probably in cahoots with Ringo. So, there was nothing to do but try to get back the missing cattle. He followed the tracks into the hills around Galeyville. Once in town, he proceeded to Ringo's headquarters, "the saloon without a name," where he was immediately accosted by the gunman who asked, "What the hell are you doing up here?" Abe did not want to give away the nature of his mission right away and stared back into Ringo's almost "baby blue" eyes. Then with a show of bravado he tossed a twenty-dollar gold piece on the bar and invited all present to drink until the money ran out, putting everyone in a good mood.

After a few rounds, Ringo returned to his original question as to what Abe was doing in Gayleyville. Abe told him about the stampede and that he was looking for his cattle. He offered to pay Ringo and his boys to round up the strays. Ringo joked for a while before getting down to business. He wanted to know why Mexican herders had not been sent up to retrieve the cattle, since he and his gang would have had a little fun before shooting them. When he saw that Abe was neither amused nor impressed by this brag, Ringo asked how much money he had. He told him one hundred dollars. Why Ringo did not just take the money, keep the cattle and dispatch Abe remains a mystery. Perhaps he admired the Kid's *chutzpah.* As it turned out, Ringo offered to round up and return the lost steers for that amount. The agreement was made, and the following day, the rustlers brought

Abraham Franklin, aka "The Kid," cowboy, businessman, banker and Graham County supervisor. *Courtesy Arizona Jewish Historical Society, Phoenix, Arizona.*

the cattle to the next watering hole. Abe got his livestock back, which he succeeded in delivering to the government, and Ringo and the boys made one hundred dollars.

After the stampede incident, Abe maintained a more or less friendly relationship with Ringo, who more than once helped out the Kid. Abe also recalled a saloon in Safford where he was being bullied by a fellow with a pistol when Ringo entered, put some money on the bar and announced that any of his or the Kid's friends could have a drink. Needless to say, everyone, including the bully, accepted the gunslinger's hospitality. On another occasion, Abe told the story of the time he was minding the Jacobs brothers store in Safford when a group of ruffians came in and began poking around the merchandise, shouting insults and generally causing a disturbance. Just then, Ringo walked in, slammed his pistol on the counter and proclaimed, "If there is going to be a row, I think I would like to be in on it." The troublemakers quickly left.

On other occasions, Abe could be on the receiving end of Ringo's high-spirited brand of fun. In 1880, Ringo, Ike Clanton and gunfighter Joe Olney (aka Joe Hill) had a dispute with a beef contractor at San Carlos and decided to vent their anger by riding down to Safford and shooting up the town. They shot out the lamps in a local saloon and then moved on to the Jacobs store, with Abe recalling that he was once again behind the counter. They put holes in "everything they fancied," forced a man named Wickersham to dance by aiming at his feet and made Abe pour drinks while laughing and stirring the cocktails with their pistol barrels. Abe must have breathed a sigh of relief when they exited the store. But things got even wilder in the street when the cowboys put fifty rounds into a nearby mill owned by Barron Jacobs and operated by his brother-in-law Marcus Katz. After thoroughly terrorizing Safford, Ringo, Clanton and Olney decided to go have another "jollification" at Solomonville. But they must have calmed down, or the drinks poured by Abe were strong enough to induce drowsiness, or maybe after Safford they ran low on ammunition. Whatever the reason, Isadore Solomon, his store and the town survived unscathed.

Although he may not have shed a tear, Abe likely felt a bit sad when Ringo died in July 1882, either of a self-inflicted gunshot or at the hands of another gunman. Abe Franklin spent a number of years ranching in southeastern Arizona. He also served as a Graham County supervisor and Maricopa County immigration commissioner and took an active role in real estate and banking as well. The Kid passed away in 1932.

Running with a Fast Crowd, Hyman Solomon

Tombstone banker Hyman Solomon should have lived a quiet life. He came to the boomtown from San Diego and for a while was a liquor dealer. He also managed the Tombstone branch of the Pima County Bank for the Jacobs brothers, who preferred employees to be conventional in their lifestyles. But Solomon preferred the controversial. He chose to fraternize openly with Wyatt, Virgil and Morgan Earp and their associate, dentist turned gambler and gunfighter John Henry "Doc" Holliday. In 1882, when Wyatt and his posse left Tombstone on the "Vendetta Ride" to seek vengeance for the assassination of Morgan and wounding of Virgil, Solomon was said to have provided an unarmed Holliday with his own Winchester. On another occasion, Solomon's cousin, saloonkeeper Ike Levy, lost his business to Wells Fargo agent Fred Dodge in a faro game. An enraged Levy started shooting. Fortunately, his aim was as bad as his ability at cards and no one was hurt. Dodge and Solomon then had a tense meeting, which ended with the banker threatening to take back his cousin's property with shotguns. Eventually, cooler heads prevailed, and compromise was reached, allowing Levy to continue to operate his saloon. Tombstone avoided another round of bloodshed.

WYATT EARP..."A DAMN JEW BOY"?

The fact that Wyatt Earp's ashes are buried in Colma, California's Jewish Hills of Eternity cemetery is well known. But how did he get there? Earp's third wife (common law), Josephine Sara Marcus, was Jewish. Her family settled in San Francisco, but much of Josephine's life is murky. She may have been a prostitute in central Arizona under the name of Sadie Mansfield—or maybe not. She may have come to Tombstone as a member of a traveling theatrical troupe—or maybe not. Josephine was known as the mistress of Tombstone lawman and politician Johnny Behan but dumped him after meeting Wyatt. Josephine and Wyatt remained together for forty-six years. Although Wyatt certainly was not Jewish, he did have contacts in the Jewish community. Hyman Solomon reportedly helped him make bail after the shootout at the OK Corral and occasionally staked him in business ventures.

Henry Jaffa, Albuquerque merchant and friend of Wyatt Earp who stayed with him while things cooled off in Arizona following the "Vendetta Ride." *Courtesy Special Collections/Center for Southwest Research (UNM Libraries), 000-119-9.*

After the "Vendetta Ride," Wyatt went to New Mexico and stayed with a friend, Jewish merchant Henry Jaffa, first mayor of Albuquerque. During this visit, the lawman was reported to have shown respect to his host by touching the mezuzah on entering Jaffa's home. Where did he learn this? From Josephine? Doc Holliday may have resented Wyatt's spending so much time with Jaffa or had trouble with his relationship with Josephine, since while dining with him at Fat Charlie's Restaurant in Albuquerque, Holliday declared that Wyatt was becoming "a damn Jew boy." The remark so angered Earp that he got up and left the restaurant. Following this incident, the friendship cooled between the two icons of the Wild West. Wyatt and Josephine continued their life on the frontier, residing in cities, mining camps and boomtowns throughout the West and Alaska. Josephine never denied her Jewishness, and the couple may have kept the tradition of placing a mezuzah on the doors of their various residences. Wyatt also was reported to have attended at least one Passover seder with Josephine's family in San Francisco, exchanging his Stetson for a yarmulke. When Wyatt died in 1929, Josephine placed Wyatt in Hills of Eternity, where she joined him in 1944.

LINE OF DUTY

Life on the Arizona frontier could be dangerous, but those dangers increased for men who sought to bring law and order to the region. During the territorial era, a number of Jews served in law enforcement, and of these, two, in particular, paid the ultimate price. In July 1882, twenty-nine-year-old Kiv Phillips served as a deputy for Tombstone sheriff Johnny Behan. In this capacity, he attempted to arrest Filomeno Orante, who had become roaring drunk down at the Capital Saloon. Unfortunately for Kiv, everything went wrong. When he got to the Capital, Orante was out in the street and pretty unsteady on his feet. Phillips attempted to disarm the drunkard, but Orante pulled out his pistol and fired, mortally wounding the deputy. The dying Phillips in turn managed to shoot his adversary in the leg and then stumbled through the saloon before collapsing. The local press praised Kiv for his bravery and good habits. His remains eventually were sent to California for burial in Hills of Eternity.

A more sinister murder took the life of Officer William "Bill" Katzenstein in 1902. A native of Sacramento, California, the thirty-four-year-old Katzenstein had been a policeman prior to moving to Tucson, where he worked as an assistant engineer with the fire department. He also joined the Tucson Police Department as a part-time officer. With dark, penetrating eyes, a precisely trimmed moustache and wearing either his tailored fire department or police uniform, Katzenstein cut a dashing figure around town. On the evening of July 28, he responded as a policeman to a fire at a store and proceeded to prevent looting. He then set aside his gun and switched to his fireman's duties. While trying to remove the cap from a fire hydrant, he was ambushed by a close friend of a man in jail for murder. The shooting was part of a plot to get revenge against Katzenstein, who had arrested the accused. Five bullets sped toward the officer. One of them struck him in the face, and he died a few minutes later. Katzenstein was survived by his wife and daughter. All of Tucson seemed to join in the mourning. The Knights of Pythias fraternal order saw to the shipment of his body back to Sacramento.

8

PIONEERING WOMEN

HANNAH MEIER—ALSO A PIONEER

In 1862, California merchant Julius Meier settled in La Paz. His store sold general merchandise as well as copper and tinware and did very well. Within a few months, Meier arranged to have his wife, Hannah, and their children join him. Their arrival must have created quite a stir at La Paz, since in early territorial Arizona, most Anglo men, like Mike Goldwater, came alone, leaving their families in California or the East. Amid the bleak surroundings, Hannah sought to make a home for her husband and children. In so doing, she became the first known Jewish woman to settle in the territory. But trying to maintain what she regarded as a proper residence amid the heat, dust, tarantulas, snakes and her roughhewn neighbors became an impossibility. She let Julius know of her displeasure in no uncertain terms. He finally decided to quit Arizona, indicating that he was doing so for the sake of his family and expressing his intention to find some place with "better scools [sic] and society."

SOCIAL NORMS AND CULTURAL CONSTRAINTS

For the next five decades, other Jewish women would follow Hannah Meier to the Arizona Territory. Many would stay. Most came as wives, sisters, cousins and daughters of men seeking their fortunes. Unlike their Gentile sisters, however, these women brought with them not only the social norms of nineteenth-century America but also millennia of Jewish religious, social and cultural laws and traditions that governed their conduct and roles in and out of the home. While they lacked most civil rights, women had a "social mission" to transmit cultural, moral and religious values to their families. Although society recognized the need for a few women and girls, especially widows and orphans, to seek employment, the lines of work that they could pursue were limited. In general, women could not be economic competitors to men.

Jewish tradition recognized the importance of women in supporting the family both morally and economically. Working alongside husbands, fathers and brothers when necessary was expected. During the late nineteenth and early twentieth centuries, however, the status of women in both Jewish and Gentile cultures began to change. This change allowed increased economic

Like a number of Jewish women, Sarah Goldwater did not like living on the frontier. To visit his wife, Mike had to journey to San Francisco. *Courtesy Distinctive Collections, BMG-AMP-002, Arizona State University Library, Tempe, Arizona.*

activity and participation by women in social, charitable and political causes outside of the home. Within the Jewish community, the improvement in the status of women was one aspect of a more liberal Judaism that incorporated increased participation in religious activities, wider educational opportunities and greater opportunities for work and service.

To this changing social, cultural and religious environment, territorial Arizona added the catalyst of the frontier. The frontier meant freedom from some traditional constraints, as well as living in a rigorous and occasionally dangerous environment. In Arizona, Jewish pioneers could face isolation from family and friends, the mainstream of Jewish life and, at times, Anglo-European society altogether. Some women, such as Sarah Goldwater, did not stay long. She had had enough of frontier life and chose to return to California at the first available opportunity. If Michel wanted her company, he would have to get on the stagecoach and steamer (or later the train) to San Francisco.

Coming to the Territory

Prior to the arrival of the railroad, women made the journey to their Arizona homes by wagons or stagecoaches, enduring the dangers and discomforts inherent in such conveyances. Most came with their husbands, parents or siblings. Rosa Katzenstein Drachman, the young bride of Tucson merchant Philip Drachman, fresh from the East Coast, took in stride the perils and inconveniences of the trip in a four-horse ambulance from San Bernardino, California, to Tucson in the fall of 1868. In later years, she recalled:

> *The first night we camped out I could not sleep on account of the howling of the coyotes. The horses were tied to the side of the wagon. Our bedding was spread on the ground, and that is the way we slept. When we were ready to start in the morning, I looked for my sunbonnet, which was made of straw with a ruffle of gingham, all I could find was the ruffle—the horses had eaten the straw. Had to wear a bandana handkerchief on head. Bought hat at Yuma—was a sight. Big straw hat with immense roses trimmed all around. They were all colors. It was the best I could get.*

As they neared Tucson, she noted:

> *On the ground at the stage station was lying a man who had been wounded by the Apaches. The Apaches were very bad in those days. After a long and tedious journey across the desert, where there was nothing but cactus, sand and brush until my eyes would ache at seeing nothing but the immense freight teams which they called "Arizona Schooners," and mighty glad we were to see them, we reached Tucson.*

For others, overland travel could be a more harrowing experience. Anna Freudenthal Solomon recalled the trip she made with her husband, Isadore, and their children from Las Cruces, New Mexico, to Pueblo Viejo (later Solomonville) in the Gila valley in the 1870s:

> *When we were going to leave Las Cruces we bought a two seated wagon, called a buckboard, and a pair of horses. Into this we put our tent, some bedding, our kitchen utensils, our provisions, our clothes, our children and ourselves. It took us several days and nights to get there. But, oh, how frightened I was thinking I saw Indians. I did not expect to get here alive with our children. Just before we reached this place, we heard a dreadful*

noise that Indians make when they are on the warpath....When we were almost home, the Mexicans told us that it was a coyote.

Relatively few Jewish women came to Arizona in as arduous and scary a manner as did Rosa Drachman and Anna Solomon. Young women, particularly those from the East, however, must have been a bit cautious when their Arizona husbands led them to the territory. Julia Frank did not know what she was getting into when she married the Irrepressible Z in New York City in October 1875. Following a transcontinental train trip/ honeymoon, the couple traveled to San Diego to begin the desert crossing to Arizona. On the day of their departure, William came bounding down the hotel steps with two bandoliers across his chest, a brace of pistols around his waist, and carrying a rifle—a perfect outfit, he indicated, for travel to the territory. Julia may have been surprised, but she took her husband's display in stride, as she did when informed that the stagecoach before theirs had been held up.

Most Jewish women did not arrive in Arizona until the 1880s, when completion of the Southern Pacific and Santa Fe railroads connected the territory with the East and West Coasts. This made travel to the territory both easier and safer and encouraged bachelors to leave Arizona to find brides. The railroads also brought more families as well as single Jewish women who eventually would become the wives of lonely Arizonans. But what was life like for these pioneering women?

New Home in the New Land

Whether traveling alone or with a new husband, with a family, by wagon or steamcar, the reaction of most newcomers arriving in the territory was one of surprise and often dismay. The land, flora, fauna, people and customs of nineteenth-century Arizona could be unfamiliar to immigrants from California and totally alien to those from the East or Europe. In Tucson, even the prominent families lived in dirt-floor adobes. Pioneer Leo Goldschmidt described such a residence:

We lived in adobe rooms, ceiled with cloth, if there was a ceiling, no baths, lights or conveniences of any kind. We carried our water from a well, our fuel from where we could get it and our commodities came the long trip overland by ox team or mule team until after the railroad finally arrived in Tucson.

William Zeckendorf and family pose for a photograph. Despite the genteel screen behind them, a rough adobe wall can be seen in the background. *Courtesy Arizona Historical Society, #12615, Tucson, Arizona.*

Is it any wonder that recent arrivals such as Rosa Drachman and Anna Solomon greeted their new homeland with tears? Despair, however, gave way to a resolve to build a life in the territory for themselves and their families. Rosa overcame the novelty of being one of only a handful of Anglo women and living in a Mexican pueblo where most men openly carried firearms. Anna soon recovered from the initial shock over her surroundings and settled into making a comfortable home for her husband, family and travelers who found themselves in the remote village of Solomonville.

For the majority of Jewish women in territorial Arizona, life revolved around home and family, and large families were not unusual. Among those with limited incomes, this meant a never-ending routine of cooking, washing, cleaning and mending, punctuated by illness and the occasional death of a child. By and large, however, most Jews belonged to the territory's merchant (middle and upper-middle) class, and many housewives could hire help to relieve them of some of the more arduous domestic chores. Although these women still had the responsibility for managing the household, and certainly did not lead a life free from the specters of illness and premature death, when their children could attend local or boarding schools, they had some amount of time for activities outside the home.

BUSINESSWOMEN

For many years, work outside the home for women meant the traditional professions of teaching or nursing. A small number of Jewish women in territorial Arizona also entered into businesses. Many did this to support their families because of the death, illness or insolvency of their husbands or when he had too many other business matters to attend to. When saloonkeeper and cigar store owner Philip Drachman died suddenly in November, 1889, his widow and children kept the businesses going. The wife of Tucson merchant Henry Welisch once took over the business to shelter her husband's assets from persistent creditors. Women often worked behind the counters with their husbands in stores and shops. In the early years of their life in the Gila valley, Anna Solomon minded the store (in addition to maintaining their house and raising the children) while Isadore worked at the charcoal business. Although such situations may have drawn criticism from those who believed in the man as sole provider, the notion of a wife "pitching in" to help out had long been established in Jewish tradition. Some

Solomon Hotel, Solomonville, Arizona, Gila Valley.

When Anna and Isadore Solomon added a second story to their original Solomonville store, they turned it into a hotel with Anna as hotel keeper. *Courtesy Arizona Jewish Historical Society, Phoenix, Arizona.*

women also sought to gain economic independence as entrepreneurs, or "sole traders," working outside the home for their own income.

A common business for women was running a boardinghouse or small hotel. In the 1880s, Mrs. Jake Abraham ran her husband's Clifton hotel, and after the turn of the century a Mrs. Cohn took in lodgers in Phoenix. By far, however, the most notable Arizona hostelry maintained by a Jewish woman belonged to Anna Solomon. The hotel was located in the Solomon store and home. Since the town lacked a formal lodging house, the Solomons began taking in travelers. Anna kept the hotel, described by one visitor as containing "valuable rugs and Indian blankets, a collection of good pictures, a piano, and a library of which many a city dweller would be proud." She did not issue keys to guests, having enough confidence in the honesty of her clientele to make locks unnecessary. There were no reported incidents of her trust being betrayed. The price of a night's lodging, which included meals, came to one dollar. Cuisine consisted of liberal servings of fresh meat and vegetables prepared by Mrs. Solomon and her Chinese cook and served by Mexican waiters. Hotel guests shared the table with the Solomon family, neighbors, soldiers, cattlemen and travelers. A relaxing evening of music and conversation in the Solomon parlor usually followed. Anna and her hotel brought comfort, culture and gastronomic excellence to the Arizona frontier.

Another common line of work for women in the territory was ladies' tailoring. Beginning with Mrs. David Levy, who established a "fashionable dressmaker, cutter and fitter shop" at her Prescott residence in 1876, Jewish women operated ladies' tailoring and millinery businesses in Phoenix and Tucson. A Mrs. Gothelf maintained the exclusive French Millinery Shop that catered to the upper crust of Tombstone society. By the dawn of the twentieth century, women's employment opportunities had begun to improve as Arizona's demand for teachers and nurses increased and "white collar" jobs as secretaries, salesclerks and cashiers opened up. Of course, not all women took up these usual female occupations. In Bisbee, for example, Lena Rosenstern kept a pawnshop, while in Douglas, Mrs. I.B. Cohn was a dealer in secondhand goods.

PROSTITUTION

Evidence of Jewish prostitutes in territorial Arizona is scarce, but there may well have been some, particularly in mining towns. In the 1870s, Josephine Sarah Marcus may have been a dance hall entertainer and engaged in prostitution under the name Sadie Mansfield. Newspapers reported winter arrivals in Phoenix, Tucson and other desert communities of destitute single Jewish women. Often health seekers, if desperate enough, turned to prostitution. Brothels were present in most of the larger towns and cities, as were red-light districts like Tucson's Wedge and Maiden Lane. During the 1890s, Phoenix tailor Henry Rosenstein made frequent court appearances on charges of maintaining a "disorderly house," a polite euphemism for a bordello, and cavorting with the city's demimonde. In the early twentieth century, Lithuanian-born Harry Friedman, a stout, busy one-armed optician and jeweler, complained strongly to the U.S. Department of Justice about the importation into Salt River valley of immigrant Jewish girls for immoral purposes. Newspaper accounts of the charges, however, never provided evidence of his complaints. The possibility of Jewish women entering the world's oldest profession, however, did worry Jews in the major towns and cities. Beginning in the 1880s, both Jewish and Gentile civic and charitable organizations sought to assist women down on their luck to prevent them from falling into prostitution. Arizona officially outlawed prostitution in 1918, six years after statehood.

PARTIES, PARTIES!

On the lighter side, during the late nineteenth and early twentieth centuries, Jewish women who did not need employment outside the home still had a number of activities to occupy their time. Social, cultural, educational and service organizations existed in the territory's principal towns. Jewish and Gentile elites mingled during the social seasons at teas, "tally ho," "tacky" and "kindergarten" parties as well as other harmless entertainments in imitation of the upper crusts of the Pacific and Atlantic coasts. Among the Jewish population, organizations such as Tucson's Lotus and Myrtle clubs celebrated birthdays, engagements and weddings during the 1880s. The Purim holiday, which commemorates the biblical Queen Esther, was usually observed with banquets and dancing parties attended by both Jews and Gentiles. At Tucson's first Purim Ball in 1886, Jennie Migel Drachman, the wife of cigar store owner Sam Drachman, dressed as a tamale vendor and offered a rendition of the Tamale Girl song to the delight of those in attendance. The Phoenix 1884 Purim Ball, hosted by Mrs. Charles Goldman, drew twenty-one ladies, about half of whom were Jewish, and thirty-seven men, of whom twenty-three were Jews. Despite this gender imbalance, a good time must have been had by all, since the dancing, games and other amusements lasted until 3:00 a.m.

Frivolity did not mark all the social activities of Arizona's Jewish women. Mrs. David Levy and Mrs. Louis Wollenberg took leading roles in Prescott's Chautauqua Reading Club during the 1880s and 1890s. The occasional piano recitals given by Mrs. Nathan Ellis of Prescott developed during the 1880s into public concerts enjoyed by the whole town. In 1907, Madeline Heineman, the wife of Tucson liquor and cigar merchant Simon Heineman, helped establish the Saturday Morning Music Club. At first, the twelve women involved gathered to perform for their own entertainment. Four years later, however, the Music Club invited popular opera singer Frieda Langendorf to present a concert in Tucson, and Madeline Heineman shouldered most of the work of organizing what turned out to be a very popular event.

CHARITY

During the late nineteenth century, charitable activities were considered socially and morally acceptable for women. In November 1893, community leader Jennie Migel Drachman issued a call to the "leading women" of Tucson to meet at her home to form a charitable organization. The result of this gathering was the establishment of the Woman's Universal Benevolent Association of Tucson. Although participation was not limited to Jews, the association drew many of its members from the Jewish elite. The objective of the organization was to aid the "worthy poor" of the community. The association divided the town into quarter sections and assigned a visiting committee to each, providing the less fortunate with employment references, food, clothing, medical care and education. To support these projects, the women undertook a number of fundraising efforts, the most popular being costume parties. The association continued its good works through the turn of the twentieth century, with Henrietta Jacobs, Mrs. Hugo Zeckendorf and Therese Ferrin serving as officers. On her own, Therese Ferrin also acted as a voluntary nurse, although prior to her marriage, she had been a milliner. She treated the poor without charge and gained a reputation as the "Angel of Tucson." During the late nineteenth and early twentieth centuries, Therese, along with a number of other Jewish women in Tucson, joined in forming the Hebrew Ladies Benevolent Society. In addition to its raising money for a synagogue, the society provided charitable services to needy Jewish and Gentile families alike.

While only a few individuals, such as the flamboyant Josephine Sarah Marcus Earp, have received much notice from writers of popular histories, Jewish women during Arizona's territorial period gained prominence through their talents and determination to better their communities. Their influence spread from the home to the workplace and the social, cultural and charitable activities of Arizona cities and towns. If historian Joseph Rader Marcus is correct in his statement that "without the American Jewess, there is very little American Jewish historical experience," then certainly the development of the Arizona Jewish community depended to a great extent on the presence and efforts of these pioneering women.

9

JUDAISM IN THE DESERT

STAYING JEWISH ON THE ARIZONA FRONTIER

The Jews who settled Arizona were a diverse lot, drawn to the territory for a variety of reasons. In Arizona, these pioneers encountered a range of subtle and not-so-subtle pressures that worked against maintaining Jewish religion and traditions. This proved to be true particularly among young single men who made up much of the early Jewish settlement in Arizona. Some were deeply religious and struggled to keep their traditions in a land so isolated from the mainstream of Jewish life in the United States and even from their fellow Jews on the frontier. Keeping Jewish was difficult, as no Jewish newspapers or journals in either Yiddish or English existed in Arizona. Pioneers had to subscribe to eastern or California periodicals. They observed the Sabbath and Jewish holidays as best they could but for most of the territorial period had to travel to eastern and West Coast cities with active congregations whenever possible to worship and for circumcision and bar mitzvah (coming of age ceremony) for their sons. Other Jews tried to balance business activities with religious obligations. This proved to be a problem for Jews wishing to remain observant in Arizona. Kosher foods were difficult, if not impossible, to come by, and a *shochet* (someone who could kill cattle and poultry according to Jewish law), a cantor to sing and lead the people in prayer, rabbis to teach the Torah, a *mohel* (a man learned in traditions and trained to perform circumcisions) and other practitioners of Jewish law and custom simply did not exist in early Arizona. Once again, to find these people and services, it was necessary to travel away from the territory. And then there were secular Jewish merchants who only tipped their hats to Judaism, professing not to care much one way or the other about religion, ritual or tradition. They concentrated on businesses. Such individuals might attend High Holy Days services or a Purim ball, but that would be the extent of their observances. They kept their stores open on Saturdays and Sundays and often married non-Jews. In these cases, the family would likely be lost to Judaism. Finally came the secular Jews and free thinkers, such as Nathan Appel, and even a few self-proclaimed atheists. They paid little attention to Jewish affairs and often married out of the faith.

ANTI-SEMITISM IN ARIZONA TERRITORY?

One problem territorial Arizona's Jewish population usually did not have to face was overt anti-Semitism. The immigration of Jews to the United States in the mid- and late nineteenth century did result in instances of discrimination and anti-Semitism, particularly on the East and West Coasts. This usually took the form of disparaging newspaper and magazine articles, songs, rhymes and cartoons depicting stereotypical Jews as appearing either shabbily dressed, with sinister expressions, long noses, hunched backs, beady eyes and speaking with an annoying accent, or as nouveau riche, garishly displaying their wealth. (Of course, this also was a time when German immigrants were portrayed as overweight beer guzzlers and Irish as slope-headed, beetle-browed pugilists.) On the frontier of territorial Arizona, anti-Semitic expressions, opinions and activities were not common. As throughout the West, the population usually paid little attention to the fact that many of their fellow merchants, miners, ranchers and farmers were Jewish. In Arizona, the Zeckendorfs, Goldwaters, Drachmans, Jacobs, Solomons and others were respected and considered brave settlers whose ambition and intelligence advanced growth and commerce in the territory. The fact that they were Jews just did not matter much to most Arizonans, although when Doc Holliday wanted to get a rise out of Wyatt Earp, calling him a "Jew Boy" certainly had the intended effect.

Some army officers and Indian Service officials assigned to the territory did bring preconceived stereotypical and anti-Semitic notions with them from the East. They saw Jews as parasites who manipulated prices for grain and other supplies for their own benefit and obstructed the efforts of the military in its campaigns against the Apaches and other warring tribes. Their alleged goal to keep funding from Washington flowing while not actually endangering themselves reinforced the soldiers' belief that Jews were in it for the money and not fighters. Not all officers, however, shared such a negative opinion, at least in public. After the capture and exile of Geronimo and the Chiricahua Apache, General Nelson A. Miles graciously accepted a ceremonial sword crafted by Tiffany's presented by William Zeckendorf along with the thanks of Tucson's merchants in a series of lavish events at Levin's Park and other locations. Tenth Cavalry lieutenant Powhatan Clarke also found the Jewish merchants of Tucson to be honest and most hospitable. He enjoyed their company while visiting the Old Pueblo.

One reason for their acceptance in territory's Anglo-dominated economic, political and social structures is that Jews adopted the attitudes of most other Anglo-European pioneers, particularly as regarded Native peoples and nonwhite immigrants. In large and small towns, Jews and Gentiles also mingled freely, sharing their membership in fraternal organizations such as the Masons and Odd Fellows, as volunteer firefighters, on civic boards and governing bodies and in the territorial legislature. Morris Goldwater's career, for example, included service as a Prescott city councilman as well as the city's mayor, Yavapai County supervisor, president of the territorial legislature and vice-president of the constitutional convention, as well as grand master and grand high priest of Arizona's Free and Accepted Masons and Royal Arch Masons. When someone's Jewishness was called out, as the time Charles Moses Strauss ran for mayor of Tucson and his opponent commented negatively that Strauss was a Jew, local newspapers quickly responded by saying that a person's ethnicity and religion had nothing to do with his fitness for office.

WHERE CAN I FIND A BRIDE?

One of the most perplexing problems facing Jewish men (and men comprised almost all of the territory's early Anglo-European settlers) involved marriage. It affected not only individuals but the Jewish community in general. Prior to the arrival of the transcontinental railroad lines in the territory, relatively few Jewish or Gentile women settled in Arizona. Only a handful of Jewish men, such as Isadore Solomon, brought their wives and families with them. The lack of matchmakers and marriageable Jewish women in the territory, particularly in the

In early Arizona, some Jewish men married Hispanic women. Alexander Levin wed Maria Zenona in 1867. Their children were raised as Roman Catholics. *Courtesy Arizona Historical Society, #69497, Tucson, Arizona.*

nineteenth century, compelled most single young men into one of four options. They could rely on their parents or relatives in the more settled regions of the country or Europe to arrange a marriage for them. They could journey to California, the Midwest, East Coast or Europe in search of a bride. The other alternatives would be to marry a non-Jew or take a non-Jewish mistress. A number of territorial pioneers such as Nathan Appel, Alexander Levin, "Black Jack" Newman, the Lulley brothers, all but one of Philip and Rosa Drachman's ten children and Baron Goldwater did this. Finally, they could remain bachelors, as did Leo Goldschmidt.

Laisons with Mexican women were not uncommon among Anglo bachelors in early Tucson, and some married men maintained separate households. For Jewish families, such relationships caused discord and often led to their descendants no longer practicing Judaism or identifying as having a Jewish heritage. Even Barron Jacobs had an ongoing relationship with a young Mexican woman.

Barron and his sweetheart did not keep their relationship a secret. They strolled about town, visiting Levin's

Henrietta "Yetta" Jacobs about 1900. She came to Arizona as the teenage bride of Barron Jacobs and later became bookkeeper for the family business. *Courtesy Arizona Historical Society, #40527, Tucson, Arizona.*

Park and dining at the better restaurants. When in her company, Barron lived a more settled life. He stopped frequenting the Wedge and other pleasure resorts, but his brother, and particularly his father, disapproved of his companion. Lionel and Mark did not agree on much, but they did conclude that this situation could not continue. She was not Jewish, and there was no question that Barron would marry within the faith. Barron, however, continued the relationship and fathered a child. Something had to be done, so Mark arranged a marriage between twenty-nine-year-old Barron and Henrietta "Yetta" Katz, a sixteen-year-old Jewish girl from New York. Barron had no choice. After the wedding, he stopped seeing his Mexican girlfriend, although he did continue to support their child. For her part, Yetta quickly adapted to being the wife of one of Tucson's leading businessmen. She was popular in Tucson society and did important work as bookkeeper for L.M. Jacobs & Company. Brother Lionel, however, remained a bachelor. Although he enjoyed the company of ladies in both Tucson and San Francisco, he would not marry until 1909 at age sixty-nine.

Once the tracks connected the territory with the rest of the country, however, the situation improved. Merchant Mannie Lowenstein, a cousin of Toby Czerwinsky, noted in his diary for 1883 that several marriageable Jewish women had taken up residence in Tucson, including "two Miss Cohns, Miss Czerwinsky, three Miss Gotthelfs, two Miss Goldtrees, two Miss Browns, two Miss Shuyers, Miss Wolf, Miss Elliot, Miss Ezekiel, Miss Kauffman, and Miss Laventhal." Of these, a number would soon marry Jewish men. Only rarely did Jewish women marry outside of the faith. Throughout the territorial period, however, intermarriage remained a hazard for Arizona's Jewish community.

Hometown "Rabbis"

Late on a warm afternoon in September 1873, a group of Jewish merchants in Tucson quietly locked the doors to their businesses, placing signs in the windows that they would be closed the following day. The men made their way along the dusty streets past saloons, restaurants and offices to a private home. At sundown, they began the celebration of Yom Kippur, the Day of Atonement and the holiest day of the year in the Judaic calendar. Their *minyan* (a quorum of ten men needed to carry out religious obligations) would observe Yom Kippur with fasting and prayer led by one of their number. Over the next few years, similar activities took place in Prescott and Phoenix. Jews also gathered to celebrate Rosh Hashanah, the Jewish New Year, with prayer and eating of symbolic foods (if they could get them in Arizona). Festivities for the holiday also included occasional entertainment, as in Tucson during the nineteenth century where a choir composed largely of women performed and those assembled listened to a lecture on the importance of the day. In 1895, at Nogales, the small Jewish community and invited Gentile guests enjoyed what the local newspaper hailed as a "joyous polyglot time" at Rosh Hashanah that featured a banquet, toasts, speeches and the usual musical program. This even included a stirring rendition of "The Tamale Man" (obviously popular at Jewish celebrations). Whether solemn or frivolous, these events nevertheless typified the early days of Jewish religious and cultural life in the Arizona Territory.

Judaism came west during the California gold rush of 1849 through the 1850s. Congregations of Orthodox, Reform and Conservative Jews formed in San Francisco and Los Angeles as well as towns in the Mother Lode. When merchants from these communities ventured across the Colorado River in the 1860s, they brought their religion and traditions with them, but initially their numbers were few, and they were scattered throughout the territory. Finding enough interested adult males in any one place to form a minyan proved to be a challenge. As a result, many Jews retained their relationships to congregations in California, where their families resided, while others kept their ties to the East and Midwest.

By the mid-1870s, a sufficient number of Jews had settled in Prescott, Phoenix and Tucson that worship could be conducted locally. Because there were no ordained rabbis in Arizona throughout much of the territorial period, lay religious leaders who had received a Jewish education in Europe, the East or even San Francisco performed the ceremonies. These included Nathan Ellis, David Levy and Michel and Morris Goldwater in Prescott; Sam Drachman, Isadore Gotthelf and William Zeckendorf in Tucson; and Sam and Charles Korrick, Hyman Goldberg and Selim Michaelson in Phoenix. At first, the territory's newspapers regarded the Jewish services as curiosities, but before long they reported on the dignity and solemnity of the High Holy Days observances. Held in Hebrew, sometimes with concurrent English translation, the services never failed to impress the visiting newsmen and other invited guests. Absent an ordained rabbi, local religious leaders also performed bar mitzvahs, funerals and weddings, although because the officiants had no legal status, a couple seeking to get married had to have a civil ceremony to make the union valid.

In addition to the High Holy Days, Arizona Jews celebrated other holidays, particularly Passover. Some community Passover seders were held, although many such observances took place in private homes. Non-Jews were invited to Purim celebrations, which frequently had more of a festive than religious air about them. Once again, newspapers commented positively on Purim and other observances, which usually featured a lavish meal, music and dancing.

By the 1880s, attendance at religious and secular celebrations in Prescott, Phoenix and Tucson had increased to where they could no longer be accommodated in private homes. Community leaders began renting halls for the High Holy Days and other observances. Usually, the halls were located on the upper floors of commercial buildings and belonged to the Masons or Odd Fellows, since many Jews belonged to these and other fraternal organizations. This arrangement generally worked well and provided ample room for officiants, worshippers and observers. In Phoenix in October 1897, a notice was circulated that those attending the Yom Kippur observance needed to arrive at the Elks Lodge by 6:00 p.m. The hall had to be free later that evening so the Elks could hold their regular meeting.

A Congregation in the Town Too Tough to Die

Although Jews were among the first settlers in Prescott, Tucson and Phoenix, one of the territory's earliest Jewish organizations appeared in Tombstone. As early as September 1881, a group of men known as the Tombstone Hebrew Association had been formed to locate a suitable location for High Holy Days services. Led by tailor Samuel Black, the Hebrew Association consisted largely of merchants recently arrived from California. They brought with them a longing for fellowship and a desire to worship even in as remote a place as Tombstone. One of the first priorities of the Hebrew Association was the establishment of a cemetery. This was a communal enterprise, with all Jews asked to donate to its purchase and support. It was important to locate a proper plot that could be consecrated so that each member of the community would be afforded a proper burial in line with Jewish law.

During its short life, the Tombstone Hebrew Association oversaw a number of funerals and burials as well as the transportation of remains to families outside of Arizona. It also arranged for High Holy Days services and other religious and cultural activities. After 1882, however, it began losing members as Tombstone's mining activity declined and the population dwindled. By the middle of the decade, so many had left Tombstone that the Association no longer held regular meetings or conducted services.

TUCSON'S JEWS GET TOGETHER (FOR A WHILE)

As Tombstone's Jewish community declined in the 1880s, interest in Judaism was on the rise in Tucson. Both social groups, such as the Myrtle Club, and religious and cultural organizations came into existence. Composed of men and women from the town's Jewish elite, the Myrtle Club's activities consisted mostly of dance parties, picnics and musicales, which fostered a sense of community but did little to promote religious and cultural observances. In 1880, following High Holy Days services at Levin's Park, a group of Tucson's leading Jewish merchants met at the home of Lionel Jacobs to try to form a congregation. The result was B'nai Israel, with Jacobs as president, Sam Drachman as vice president, L. Rosenstern as secretary and Fred Fleishman treasurer. B'nai Israel never formally incorporated, although it did hold services in the home of Julius Wittelshoefer.

On January 7, 1883, a number of the men who had been involved with B'nai Israel met in the Tucson Masonic Hall to inaugurate Arizona Lodge No. 337, Independent Order of B'nai B'rith. Deriving its name from the Hebrew "Sons of the Covenant," the male-only B'nai B'rith began in New York as a mutual benefit project among Jewish immigrants, but over the years it evolved into a social and philanthropic organization. Through its dues, the lodge provided health and death benefits to its members and support for community charities, as well as offering fellowship and activities such as billiards and card playing. By the 1880s, it had adapted the rituals and customs of other fraternal groups such as the Masons. The Tucson lodge prospered for a few years, holding entertainments and encouraging participation in religious observances. During this period, Abraham Marx, Sam Drachman, Gabriel Einstein, Albert E. Jacobs, Julius Wittelshoefer and William Florsheim served as presidents of the lodge. But as the decade wore on, interest in both the congregation and lodge waned, probably because of a general economic decline occasioned by southern Arizona's reduced mineral production. Merchants felt it more prudent to tend to their businesses than to religious and community functions. B'nai Israel ceased to be active after 1881, and eight years later, it became necessary for the eight remaining members of Arizona No. 337 of B'nai B'rith to consolidate with Orange Lodge No. 334 of Los Angeles.

Women Take the Initiative

While the men tried to keep the Arizona Lodge and B'nai Israel going, the Jewish women of Tucson were also busy. In 1884, they established the Hebrew Ladies Benevolent Society. In so doing, the ladies of Tucson mirrored community and philanthropic work by Jewish women in cities and towns throughout the West during the late nineteenth century. Led by Minna Czerwinsky, the wife of general merchant Toby Czerwinsky, with Eva Mansfeld, whose husband, Jacob, ran the town's book and stationery store, as vice-president; Julia Zeckendorf, wife of William Zeckendorf, as treasurer; and Mrs. William Florsheim as secretary, the society had twenty-one members. In addition to the leadership, membership read like a who's who of Tucson's Jewish community, including Mrs. Joseph Goldtree, Mrs. Isador Goldtree, Mrs. H. Schoenholtz, Mrs. G. Kresham, Mrs. I. Kauffman, Mrs. Charles Ferrin, Mrs. Herbert Drachman, Mrs. Philip Drachman, Mrs. Albert Steinfeld, Mrs. Albert E. Jacobs, Mrs. Marcus Katz, Mrs. Isadore Gotthelf, Mrs. Koppel, Mrs. Wittelshoefer, Mrs. Sam Harris and Mrs. Sondheim. They had as their objective "aiding the needy in times of distress" among both the Jewish and Gentile populations. To accomplish this, the women undertook a number of fundraising efforts, the most popular being elegant costume balls, which Jews and non-Jews alike were invited to attend and contribute.

After 1890, as many of the pioneer women passed away, moved from the territory or became too old to participate, membership and activities of the Hebrew Ladies Benevolent Society declined. This trend continued throughout the decade, but the organization did not fold completely. Under the leadership of Therese Ferrin, it became active once again in the early twentieth century. In 1900, the women were instrumental in establishing Tucson's Jewish cemetery and cemetery association to manage it. Beginning in March 1904, the Benevolent Society's name changed to the Hebrew Ladies' Aid Society, and it took on, in addition to charitable work, the task of acquiring the funds needed for a permanent house of worship. The society redoubled its fundraising efforts through even more balls, teas and bake and craft sales. The society took a major step in this direction in the early 1900s, when the women acquired property in the 500 block of as yet unpaved South Stone Avenue for a synagogue.

A Circuit Riding Rabbi Comes to Town

Establishing a synagogue with a permanent congregation, and a rabbi to lead it, had been an unrealized goal of Tucson's Jewish community since the 1880s. A men's Jewish Cemetery Benevolent Association formed and acquired a Torah, lodged in the home of Julius Wittelshofer. But the association's activities were minimal. Visitors from the East and California remarked that although the town's Jewish population was rather large, unfortunately it did not have a regular place of worship. Every year, usually after the High Holy Days, a proposal for a synagogue would come forward with much enthusiasm, but such ideas found their way to the back shelf within a few weeks. Business and other matters took precedence among the town's merchants.

In 1904, a "circuit riding rabbi," Martin Zeilonka, began visiting Tucson on behalf of the Cincinnati-based Union of American Hebrew Congregations. The union was the principal exponent of Reform Judaism in the United States. Reform Judaism originated in Germany and spread to the United States during the mid-nineteenth century. It sought to bring many of the outward appearances of Judaism into closer alignment with those of Protestant churches, including architectural appearance of synagogues, late Friday night instead of Saturday services (since most merchants kept their stores open on Saturdays), the use of diverse liturgies and prayer books, the playing of the organ at services, acceptance of "Western" music (resembling Christian hymns), mixed choirs of men and women and sermons and preaching by rabbis. Reform Judaism did not emphasize the role of ritual and regarded much of strict Jewish law adhered to by Orthodox Jews as nonbinding. This gave the individual Jew greater latitude in his or her method of worship. Such beliefs fit well in the United States and the Arizona Territory, where Jews enjoyed acceptance, mobility and freedom they had not known in Europe. Many Jews either moved frequently about the region or lived in isolation distant from established synagogues and other cultural and religious institutions. While many observant Jews still returned to California or the East, or even Europe to celebrate the holidays, others traveled to Tucson where a congregation and synagogue were in the making and the method of observance was not an issue.

Rabbi Zeilonka traveled on a lecture circuit that included Arizona, southern New Mexico and west Texas and made visits to Tucson to conduct religious services and promote the organization of a congregation. As a result, another congregation formed, with Lionel Jacobs as president, Sam Drachman as vice president, L. Rosenstern as secretary and Fred Fleishman as treasurer. With a membership of about forty, fundraising began for construction of a building on the South Stone Avenue property. Unfortunately, the new congregation did not succeed and disintegrated within a year. The ladies, however, kept raising money.

SUCCESS AT LAST!

In October 1908, following Tucson's High Holy Days observances, another attempt began to establish a synagogue. Therese Ferrin hosted a meeting of community leaders for the purpose of establishing a new congregation. She was already a leader in the Hebrew Ladies' Aid Society and was said to possess a Torah. By that December, between sixty-five and seventy-five men and their families had pledged themselves to the construction of a synagogue. The group initially called itself the Emanu-El Temple Association and began fundraising in earnest. Contributions came not only from Tucson but also from Jews as far away as Globe, Bisbee and Nogales. Planning for a structure at the South Stone Street site could now go forward under the leadership of a new organization called the Hebrew Benevolent Society. Incorporated in March 1910, with Sam Drachman as chairman, it assumed the functions of the Cemetery Association and the Hebrew Ladies' Aid Society. The latter group became the Temple Emanu-El Sisterhood. The Benevolent Society engaged a local Tucson architect, Ely Blount, to draw up the plans and received bids for construction. On June 21, these efforts bore fruit, with Masons from the local lodge performing an elaborate cornerstone-laying ceremony on South Stone Avenue for the Hebrew Temple Emanu-El.

Work on the building proceeded over the summer in the hope of having it ready for the High Holy Days. As Rosh Hashanah approached, all appeared to be going well, and the Benevolent Society hired Dr. E.M. Chapman, a rabbi from Albuquerque, to officiate at the dedication and conduct services. Almost at the last minute, however, the manufacturer of the furniture, pulpit, fixtures and carpeting sent word that there would be a delay in the delivery date. After decades, the effort to establish a permanent congregation and synagogue seemed to be stymied by a vendor! Disappointed but not discouraged, the directors of the Benevolent Society elected to proceed with the ceremony. Consequently, on Rosh Hashanah eve, October 3, 1910, in the one-story red brick structure that blended Neoclassical, Romanesque and Moorish architectural styles but remained almost devoid of amenities, Rabbi Chapman, the Jewish community

Tucson's Temple Emanu-El, the first synagogue in Arizona, opened to congregants in 1910. Today it houses the Tucson Jewish Museum and Holocaust Center. *Courtesy Arizona Jewish Historical Society, Phoenix, Arizona.*

of Tucson and a crowd of interested non-Jews dedicated the Temple Emanu-El building. They later celebrated the New Year in Arizona's first synagogue. The furniture eventually arrived, and Rabbi Chapman stayed on with a one-year $1,000 contract to guide the young congregation. Women of the community continued to do most of the educational, charitable and social services work. The religious and cultural establishment that the pioneers of the 1880s envisioned had, at last, become a reality.

Tucson's Jews now had a home. But what of the Jewish community in the territorial capital, Phoenix?

SALT RIVER VALLEY GETS A BURYING GROUND

The religious and cultural development of the Phoenix Jewish community during the territorial years followed a course similar to that of Tucson but without the false starts of the 1880s. As in the Old Pueblo, observances of the High Holy Days and other events initially took place in private homes and later rented halls. And as in Tucson, women took on a key but largely unrecognized role in keeping interest in Judaism and Jewish activities alive.

Beginning in the 1880s, laymen who had some training in Jewish law and ritual performed the ceremonies for the community. The territorial capital, however, did not have a Jewish burying ground until after the turn of the twentieth century. Prior to that, the deceased were laid to rest in the city's public cemetery, in plots belonging to fraternal organizations or shipped elsewhere for interment in a Jewish cemetery. Before his death in 1898, Michael Wormser stated frequently that he would donate land for a Jewish cemetery in Phoenix. Unfortunately, he died without leaving a written bequest, and his large estate (mostly land and cattle) entered into a lengthy probate. The executor, merchant Charles Goldman, contacted Wormser's heirs scattered about the United States and Europe about his verbal commitment and obtained agreements to give the community a plot of land south of the Salt River and west of town. On the evening of January 12, 1900, the leading Jews of the city met to form an organization to receive the property. Headed initially by merchants Charles Goldman (president), Louis Melczer (vice president), Charles Levy (secretary) and banker Simon

Established on property donated by Michael Wormser, Beth Israel Cemetery was the first permanent Jewish site in the Salt River Valley. *Courtesy Arizona Jewish Historical Society, Phoenix, Arizona.*

Oberfelder (treasurer), the group notified the heirs of the organization's existence and started the legal steps to secure the property. Burials at the site, however, began as early as 1902, before actual title to the land had been granted. The ground was there, ready for use, and how would the heirs find out anyway? Most lived a continent or an ocean away. Progress toward the clear title, nevertheless, remained stalled for another two years until 1904, when the Phoenix Hebrew Cemetery Association finally obtained the last transfer of land for the cemetery tract.

While progress on the cemetery inched along, a number of parents became concerned over the lack of Jewish education in the Salt River valley. Following a particularly well-attended Yom Kippur service in October 1903, an announcement was made that a Sabbath School for Jewish children would be organized in Phoenix. The next week, parents and children gathered in the Padget Hall and set up a program of religious services and study. The resulting Sabbath School met sporadically for the next seven years.

Time Comes for a Synagogue

Although the Phoenix community had a cemetery and Sabbath School, there was still no synagogue. Agitation for a Jewish house of worship continued. Progress toward that goal, however, was slow. In 1910, a health seeker, Rabbi Herman Hofstadter, arrived from San Francisco, prompting Phoenix Jews to take an important step toward the establishment of a permanent congregation. They formed Congregation Emanuel, with attorney Barnett Marks as president; Charles Korrick, vice president; Henry Meyers, secretary; and Mrs. Louis Melczer, treasurer. The organization would be under the leadership of Rabbi Hofstadter, who conducted Shabbat services on Friday evenings and taught a Sunday school in Melczer Hall. Congregation Emanuel began auspiciously, with twenty-one children in the Sunday school, well-attended Sabbath services and a Hanukkah program. In May 1911, the congregation held Phoenix's first recorded bar mitzvah ceremony for Peter Barnett, the son of Dr. and Mrs. C.D. Barnett.

Rabbi Hofstadter left the Salt River valley, and Congregation Emanuel suspended its activities over the summer of 1911. It attempted to begin again that fall, and that December, Rabbi Chapman of Tucson accepted an invitation to assist the Phoenix congregation in its development. He remained with the congregation into 1912 when he, too, departed the valley. Emanuel struggled along for another couple of years when

Temple Beth Israel, Phoenix's first permanent synagogue completed in 1922, and 1930 annex. Today the buildings house the Cutler-Plotkin Jewish Heritage Center. *Courtesy Arizona Jewish Historical Society, Phoenix, Arizona.*

Rabbi Emil Ellinger of Tucson agreed to help keep the movement alive, making weekly trips to Phoenix to officiate and instruct. Over the next few years, Phoenix Jews established a B'nai B'rith lodge, a chapter of the Young Men's Hebrew Association and a section of the National Council of Jewish Women. These groups worked earnestly to raise funds for the establishment of a synagogue. Jewish leaders in Phoenix also incorporated the Phoenix Hebrew Center Association with Charles Korrick as president; Sydney Wolf, secretary; and Sylvan Ganz (son of Emil Ganz), treasurer. When enough money had been raised, this group hired the prestigious Phoenix architectural firm of Lescher, Kibbey and Mahoney to design the Mission-style structure. It cost $14,000, a tidy sum in the early 1920s. The association also brought a permanent rabbi, Russian immigrant Dr. David L. Liknaitz, from Los Angeles, to oversee the completion of the synagogue. Located at Second Street and Culver, the Spanish Mission-style building called Temple Beth Israel began serving Jews of the Salt River valley in the spring of 1922. It continued doing so until 1949.

Religious Diversity

Jewish religious life in the Tucson and Phoenix congregations was necessarily diverse. Since both communities had but one congregation each, these institutions had to be sensitive to a wide range of ideas and beliefs. Some early Jewish settlers in the territory and more recently arrived immigrants tried to retain the orthodoxy then prevalent in Russia and eastern Europe. They found, however, that conditions in remote Arizona worked strongly against maintenance of their traditional customs and beliefs. The majority of the territory's Jews during the late nineteenth and early twentieth centuries, however, tended more toward Reform or Conservative Judaism. These forms of Judaism sought to maintain some or most of the theology of orthodoxy while adapting to the freer and more plural environment found in the western United States. The synagogues in both Tucson and Phoenix cast as wide a net as possible to obtain congregants. But as far as rituals were concerned, the Jews of Tucson appeared more Reform-minded and held services primarily in English, with occasional Hebrew words and phrases. The Phoenix congregation, on the other hand, offered services in both Hebrew and English.

Congregations in Douglas and Bisbee

Although Tucson and Phoenix attracted most of the Jewish immigrants to territorial Arizona, during the early twentieth century, congregations appeared in some of the smaller communities as well. The rapid growth of the smelter town of Douglas initially attracted a substantial number of Jews, primarily merchants. By 1904, these settlers had begun holding High Holy Days services in a rented hall. Soon, a movement started for a synagogue in Douglas. While no actual construction came about, Douglas Jews did establish a congregation called Sons of Israel in 1907, a name later changed to Adath Israel. This body remained in existence until 1910, after which Douglas Jews traveled to Tucson or El Paso for religious services and events. The sentiment generated in Douglas in the early twentieth century spilled over into Bisbee where, in 1907, a small congregation was formed. It did not last long, becoming more of a benevolent society. Both the Bisbee and Douglas groups, however, joined to establish a Jewish burial ground in Douglas, the Bisbee-Douglas Jewish Cemetery, located near the Mexican border in 1904.

Arizona Comes Together
for the Russian Relief Movement

During the early twentieth century, one issue attracted the interest of Jews throughout Arizona. The condition of Jews in Russia and Eastern Europe had been deteriorating since the early 1880s. Restrictive laws, Russia's infamous Pale of Settlement and organized physical attacks (pogroms) had caused many Jews to immigrate to the United States. The journey to America was both physically and emotionally taxing, but most of those who remained faced an even bleaker existence. As early as 1882, the merchants of Tucson held fundraising drives for the relief of Jews forced to leave Russia. Two decades later, newspapers throughout the territory reported in gruesome detail the violent pogroms at Kishinev and other locations in the realms of the czar. Jews in Tucson, Phoenix, Clifton, Douglas and other communities met to discuss what could be done to assist Russian Jewry in this crisis. A number of fundraising drives got underway. In Phoenix, the effort involved community leaders, including druggist Herbert Goodman and tobacco dealer Selim Michaelson, as well as Father Novatus Benzig, a prominent Roman Catholic clergyman. Lionel Jacobs coordinated activities in the southern portion of the territory. Just as with the efforts to establish congregations and build synagogues, however, while men managed the drives, women did most of the real work and raised most of the money. Renewed anti-Jewish outbreaks in the Russian Empire, following defeat in its 1904–5 war with Japan, once again prompted relief work. Responding to the pogroms and other attacks on their coreligionists, Jews throughout the territory joined in the drive. In Bisbee, the leading merchants met twice in the Pythian Hall for memorial services and raised some $250 for Jewish suffering.

Even though most Jews in territorial Arizona were of Polish, German or western European descent, they did not ignore the wave of Jewish immigration from Russia and eastern Europe to the United States in the late nineteenth and early twentieth centuries. These poor immigrants settled largely in the urban areas of the East Coast. Only a relative few made it to remote Arizona before the end of the territorial period. Many more would come later in the century. Nevertheless, through organized national charities, Arizona's Jewish community contributed to the establishment of settlement houses and other measures to assist the new arrivals in New York, Chicago and other eastern cities.

Relief efforts in early twentieth-century Arizona were significant, not so much in amounts of money raised as in the less tangible manner in which they united the territory's Jews in a common purpose. The Jewish communities of Tucson and Phoenix, which developed pretty much independently, now addressed the plight of Jews across the seas in a cooperative manner. Jews in smaller towns also experienced a rekindling of interest in Jewish cultural and religious life. The fundraising campaigns in support of coreligionists halfway around the world in the early twentieth century therefore reflected not only traditional Jewish philanthropy but also the beginning of community among the Jews of the Arizona Territory.

CONCLUDING REMARKS

Territorial Days Come to an End

By the second decade of the twentieth century, Arizona's territorial days were coming to an end. Statehood had become the main issue during the early twentieth century. Citizens in Phoenix, Tucson, Prescott and smaller communities and on farms and ranches debated Arizona's status and, in most cases, clamored for statehood. Jews were among the leaders of this statehood movement. Morris Goldwater and attorney Jacob Weinberger of Gila County served as delegates to the constitutional convention and worked hard for statehood. On February 14, 1912, Arizona was admitted to the Union as a state. On that same day, amid the parades, cheers, canon fire and other statehood celebrations, Joe Melczer married Hazel Goldberg. Children of pioneer families, they became the first Jewish couple to be wed in the new state. It was a Jewish ceremony but with an Arizona touch. The bride and groom stood under the traditional *chuppah* wedding canopy, with young Barry Goldwater, grandson of another pioneer Jew, Big Mike, and son of Baron Goldwater and a newly arrived Episcopalian, Hattie "Jo," serving as ring bearer.

Judaism and Jewish life did not die in the Arizona desert. The tenacity of Jewish men and women to maintain their religion, traditions and customs overcame secular influences of the frontier. Staying, or trying to stay kosher; traveling to Los Angeles, San Francisco or New York to become bar mitzvah; finding a Jewish bride; placing mezuzahs on the doorposts; or marrying under the chuppah, Jews remained Jews, as much as the frontier conditions of the territory allowed. They laid a firm foundation for the vibrant community that developed in the twentieth century and beyond.

BIBLIOGRAPHY

Manuscript Collections

Arizona Corporation Commission. Phoenix, Arizona. Articles of Incorporation. Cochise County Bank.

———. Articles of Incorporation. Phoenix Hebrew Center Association.

———. Articles of Incorporation. Solomon Commercial Company.

Arizona Department of Library, Archives and Public Records. Phoenix, Arizona. Arizona Territorial Superintendent of Public Instruction, Biennial Report, Tucson, January 1, 1889.

———. Biography Clipping File, Emil Ganz.

Arizona Historical Society Library. Tucson, Arizona. Appel, Nathan B. Reminiscence.

———. Cruse, Thomas. "My Reminiscences of Army Life."

———. Drachman, Harry A. Papers. "Recollections of Old Tucson."

Arizona State University. Digital Repository. Tempe, Arizona. Hayden Pioneer Biographies.

Arizona State University Library. Greater Arizona Collection. Tempe, Arizona. Brooks, William Eugene Collection.

———. Ridgway, Ryder Collection.

California State Library. California History Section. Sacramento, California. Ephraim W. Morse Collection.

Clarke Collection. St. Louis, Missouri. No. A0293.

Franklin Family Collection. Goldbaum, Julius. Records.

Goldwater Collection.

Harvard University. Business School. Baker Library. Special Collections. Cambridge, Massachusetts. Dun and Bradstreet, Inc. Credit Ledgers. Western Territories.

Hebrew Union College. American Jewish Archives. Cincinnati, Ohio. Apple, James. "The Economic History of the Jews of the Southwestern United States as Found in the Fireman Papers." (typescript).Huntington Library. San Marino, California. Abel Stearns Papers.

Jacobs Family Business Records.

Jacobs Family Collection.

Leo Baeck Institute for Jewish History. New York, New York. Schuster, Helen, "The Adolph Schuster Family." Interview with Norton Stern, July, 1972. (typescript).

National Archives. Washington, D.C. Records of Posts. 393.7. Records of United States Continental Commands, 1821–1940. RG 393.

———. Registers of Beef and Fresh Meat Contracts. Records of the Office of the Commissary General of Subsistence, 1818–1913. RG 92.

———. Registers of Contracts. Records of the Quartermaster General, 1774–1985. RG92. Records of the U.S. and Mexico Claims Commission. Claim No. 506. N.B. Appel v. Mexico. RG 76.

Northern Arizona University. Special Collections. Flagstaff, Arizona. B. Schuster Company Records.

Sharlot Hall Museum/Library. Prescott, Arizona. Obituary Files.

Temple Beth Israel Library. Phoenix, Arizona. Memorandum from the Phoenix Chapter of the Council of Jewish Women, October 30, 1921.

University of Arizona Library. Special Collections. Tucson, Arizona. Appel, Nathan B. Biographical Sketch.

———. Bloom Southwest Jewish Archives.

———. Certificate of Incorporation. La Providencia Silver Mining Company.

———. Franklin, Selim Papers.

———. "Franklin Tells of Stampede in Herding Cattle." (undated clipping).

———. Jacobs Family Papers. Temple Emanu-El, Tucson, Arizona Fortieth Anniversary, 1910–1950 (pamphlet).

University of California, Berkeley. Bancroft Library. Berkeley, California. Bancroft Dictations, Arizona. Bancroft Scraps, Arizona.

Interviews

Korrick, Edgar. Phoenix, Arizona. December 1, 1976.
Ramenofsky, Mrs. A.I. Phoenix, Arizona. June 9, 1980.

United States Government Documents

Raymond, Rossiter W. *Mineral Resources of the States and Territories West of the Rocky Mountains.* Washington, D.C.: Government Printing Office, 1869.

Reports of the Commissioner of Indian Affairs to the Secretary of the Interior for the Years 1878–1884. Washington, D.C.: Government Printing Office, 1878–84.

U.S. Congress. Senate. *Federal Census. Territory of New Mexico and Territory of Arizona. Excerpts from the Decennial Federal Census, 1860 for Arizona County in the Territory of New Mexico, the Special Territorial Census of 1864 Taken in Arizona, and the Decennial Federal Census, 1870 for the Territory of Arizona.* S. Doc. 13. 89th Cong. 1st Sess. Washington, D.C.: Government Printing Office, 1965.

U.S. War Department. *Regulations for the Army of the United States, 1889.* Washington, D.C.: Government Printing Office, 1889.

Arizona Territorial Documents

Arizona Territorial Livestock Sanitary Board. *Brands and Marks of Cattle, Horses, Sheep, Goats and Hogs as they Appear in the Office of the Live Stock Sanitary Board of Arizona At Phoenix, Arizona.* Phoenix, AZ: Live Stock Sanitary Board of Arizona, 1908.

Biennial Report of the Superintendent of Public Instruction of the Territory of Arizona, 1890. Phoenix, AZ: Republican Book and Job Print, 1890.

Biennial Report of the Territorial Auditor to the Governor of the Territory of Arizona for the Years 1887–1888. N.p.: John J. Hawks, Auditor, 1888.

Journal of the First Legislative Assembly of the Territory of Arizona. Prescott, AZ, 1865.

"The Superintendent of Indian Affairs, Arizona Territory, Annual Reports, 1871 and 1872 (Part 1)." *Western States Jewish History* 22, no. 4 (1990).

County Documents

Claims and Deeds. La Paz. Book 1. Yuma County Recorder's Office, Yuma.

Deeds. Books 1 and 2. Maricopa County Recorder's Office, Phoenix.

Great Register of Pima County. September 27, 1880.

Maricopa County Deeds. Vol. 59. Maricopa County Recorder's Office, Phoenix.

Mining Claims. Castle Dome District. Book "A," 1863. Yuma County Recorder's Office, Yuma.

Miscellaneous Records. La Paz. Book 1. Yuma County Recorder's Office, Yuma.

1904 Great Register, Yavapai County, Territory of Arizona. Prescott, AZ: Morning Courier, 1904.

Guides, Directories and Mercantile Reference Books

A.P. Skinner's Phoenix City and Maricopa County Directory (Arizona), 1905–06. Phoenix, AZ: A.P. Skinner, Publisher, 1905.

Arizona Business Directory. Denver, CO: Gazetteer Publishing Co., 1908.

Barter, G.W. *Directory for the City of Tucson for the Year 1881.* San Francisco, CA: H.S. Crocker Co., 1881.

City of Tucson General and Business Directory for '99–'00. N.p.: Chas. T. Connelly, 1899.

Colorado, New Mexico, Utah, Nevada, Wyoming and Arizona Business Directory, 1884–1885. Chicago: R.L. Polk & Co., 1884.

Disturnell, W.C. *Arizona Business Directory and Gazetteer.* San Francisco, CA: Bacon & Co., 1881.

Hamilton, Patrick. *The Resources of Arizona.* San Francisco, CA: A.L. Bancroft & Co., 1884.

J.C. Freeman & Co. *1903–1904 Official City and Business Directory, Prescott, Arizona.* Prescott, AZ: Journal-Miner Co., 1903.

McKenney, L.M. *McKenney's Business Directory of the Principal Towns of Central and Southern California, Arizona, New Mexico, Southern Colorado and Kansas.* Oakland, CA: Pacific Press, 1882–83.

Mercantile Agency. *Reference Book (and Key) Containing Ratings of Merchants, Manufacturers and Traders Generally Throughout the United States and Canada.* New York: R. G. Dun & Co., 1908.

————. *Reference Book (and Key) Containing Ratings of the Merchants, Manufacturers and Traders Generally Throughout the United States and Canada, July, 1871.* Boston: E. Russell & Co., 1871.

Mercantile Reports from the Mercantile Agency of Hope, McKillop & Co. San Francisco, CA: Bowden & Forbes, 1872.

Meyer, A. Leonard. *Meyer's Business Directory of the City of Phoenix, Arizona, 1888.* N.p., 1888.

Phoenix City and Salt River Valley Directory. Los Angeles, CA: Arizona Directory Company, 1912.

Phoenix City and Salt River Valley Directory, 1919. Los Angeles, CA: Arizona Directory Company, 1919.

The Phoenix Directory Co.'s City Directory for the Year 1897. Phoenix, AZ: Phoenix Directory Company, Publishers, 1897.

Phoenix Directory for 1899–1900. Phoenix, AZ: Phoenix Directory Co., 1899–1900.

Sorin, T.R. *Handbook of Tucson and Surroundings.* Tucson, AZ: T.R. Sorin, Publisher, 1880.

Tucson and Tombstone General and Business Directory for 1883 and 1884. Tucson, AZ: Collier and Co., 1883.

Vaughn, Jerome H. *Resources of Graham County.* Solomonville, AZ, 1888.

Yavapai County Directory, 1913. Phoenix: Arizona Directory Company, 1913.

Newspapers

American Israelite (Cincinnati, OH), 1871–90, 1904–7.

Arizona Champion (Flagstaff), 1886–91.

Arizona Citizen (Tucson), 1879–82.

Arizona Daily Journal-Miner (Prescott), 1903.

Arizona Enterprise (Prescott), 1878.

Arizona Gazette (Phoenix), 1881–1920.

Arizona Republican (Phoenix), 1890–1920.

Arizona Sentinel (Yuma), 1872–82.

Arizona Star (Tucson), 1875–81.

Arizona Weekly Citizen (Tucson), 1882–89.

Arizona Weekly Journal-Miner (Prescott), 1885–90.

Arizona Weekly Miner (Prescott), 1873–77.

Arizona Weekly Star (Tucson), 1878–80, 1891–92.

Boston (MA) Daily Globe, 1878.

Boston (MA) Post, 1876.
Clifton (AZ) Clarion, 1883–89.
Daily Alta California (San Francisco), 1860–63.
Daily Evening Bulletin (San Francisco), 1858–65.
Daily Phoenix (AZ) Herald, 1885–91.
Douglas (AZ) Daily Dispatch, 1903–5.
El Paso (TX) Daily Times, 1894.
Graham County Bulletin. Special Illustrated Editions (Solomonville, AZ), 1897, 1900.
Holbrook (AZ) Argus, 1900–1902.
Los Angeles (CA) Star, 1861–62.
Los Angeles (CA) Times, 1901.
Mesilla (AZ) Times, 1860–61.
Mohave County Miner (Mineral Park, AZ), 1883.
Oasis (Nogales, AZ), 1894–1905.
Phoenix (AZ) Herald, 1878–85.
Prescott (AZ) Courier, 1883.
Prescott (AZ) Weekly Courier, 1883–85.
Salt River Herald (Phoenix, AZ), 1878–79.
San Diego (CA) Union, 1872–90.
San Francisco (CA) Herald, 1862.
Semi-Weekly Southern News (Los Angeles, CA), 1862.
St. John's (AZ) Herald, 1885–89.
Tombstone (AZ) Daily Nugget, 1881–82.
Tombstone (AZ) Epitaph, 1880–82.
Tri-Weekly News (Los Angeles, CA), 1863.
Weekly Arizona Miner (Prescott), 1868–86.
Weekly Arizonian (Tubac), 1859.

Contemporary Sources and Reminiscences

Altschuler, Constance Wynn, ed. *The Latest from Arizona! The Hesperian Letters.* Tucson: Arizona Pioneers Historical Society, 1969.
"Arizona Cities and Towns." *Mining and Scientific Press*, 1881.
Arizona: The New State Magazine, February 1910.
The Arizona Statewide Archival and Records Project. Division of Community Service Programs.
Bigelow, John, Jr. *On the Bloody Trail of Geronimo.* Tucson, AZ: Westernlore Press, 1986.

Browne, J. Ross. *Adventures in the Apache Country: A Tour through Arizona and Sonora with Notes on the Silver Regions of Nevada.* New York: Harper & Bros., 1871.

Chanin, Abe, and Mildred Chanin. *This Land, These Voices: A Different View of Arizona History in the Words of Those Who Lived It.* Flagstaff, AZ: Northland Press, 1977.

"Excerpts from Mose Drachman's Diary." *Arizona Sheriff*, January–February 1973.

Fireman, Bert M. "A Bar Mitzvah Message from Prescott, Arizona in 1879." *Western States Jewish Historical Quarterly*, July 1980.

Goldberg, Isaac. "An Old Timer's Experiences in Arizona." *Arizona Historical Review*, October 1929.

Goldwater, Barry M. *With No Apologies: The Personal and Political Memoirs of United States Senator Barry M. Goldwater.* New York: William Morrow & Co., 1979.

Gustafson, A.M., ed. *John Spring's Arizona.* Tucson: University of Arizona Press, 1966.

A Historical and Biographical Record of the Territory of Arizona. Chicago: McFarland & Poole, 1896.

History of Arizona Territory Showing Its Resources and Advantages: With Illustrations, Descriptive of Its Scenery, Residences, Farms, Mines, Mills, Hotels, Business Houses, Schools, Churches, etc. San Francisco, CA: Wallace W. Elliot & Co., 1884.

Lake, Carolyn, Ed. *Under Cover for Wells Fargo: The Unvarnished Recollections of Fred Dodge.* Boston: Houghton Mifflin, 1969.

Lapham, Macy. *Crisscross Trails: Narrative of a Soil Surveyor.* Berkeley, CA: Willis E. Berg, 1949.

Lesinsky, Henry. *Letters Written by Henry Lesinsky to His Son.* New York: By the Author, 1924.

Letter from Norman Simon, Executive Director, District Grand Lodge No. 4, B'nai B'rith, to the Author. Los Angeles, June 9, 1976.

Lummis, Charles. *General Crook and the Apache Wars.* Edited by Turbese Lummis Fiske. Flagstaff, AZ: Northland Press, 1966.

Marcus, Jacob R. "An Arizona Pioneer: The Memoirs of Sam Aaron." *American Jewish Archives*, October 1958.

Nicholson, John, ed. *The Arizona of Joseph Pratt Allyn, Letters from a Pioneer Judge: Observations and Travels, 1863–1866.* Tucson: University of Arizona Press, 1974.

Perkins, William. *Three Years in California: William Perkins Journal of Life at Sonora, 1849–1852.* Berkeley: University of California Press, 1964.

Proceedings of District Grand Lodge No. 5, Independent Order of B'nai B'rith. San Francisco: W.A. Woodward & Co., 1885.

Proceedings of the Twenty Fourth Annual Session of the Most Worthy District Grand Lodge No. 4, Independent Order of B'nai B'rith. San Francisco, CA: W.A. Woodward & Co., 1887.

Proceedings of the Twenty-Sixth Annual Session of the Most Worthy District Grand Lodge No. 4, Independent Order of B'nai B'rith. San Francisco, CA: Rosenthal-Saalsburg Co., 1889.

Schneiderman, Harry. *American Jewish Year Book, 5682, October 3, 1921 to September 22, 1922.* Philadelphia: Jewish Publication Society of America, 1921.

Sloan, Richard E. *Memories of an Arizona Judge.* Stanford, CA: Stanford University Press, 1932.

Stern, Norton B. *Mannie's Crowd: Emanuel Lowenstein, Colorful Character of Old Los Angeles, and a Brief Diary of the Trip to Arizona and Life in Tucson of the Early 1880s.* Glendale, CA: Arthur H. Clark Company, 1970.

Szold, Henrietta. *The American Jewish Year Book, 5667, September 20, 1906 to September 8, 1907.* Philadelphia: Jewish Publication Society of America, 1906.

———. *The American Jewish Year Book, 5668, September 9, 1907 to September 27, 1908.* Philadelphia: The Jewish Publication Society of America, 1907.

"Tombstone Notes." *Golden Era*, May 1889.

"The Vizina Mine." *Arizona Quarterly Illustrated*, January 1881.

Wister, Fanny Kimble, ed. *Owen Wister Out West: His Journals and Letters.* Chicago: University of Chicago Press, 1958.

Wollenberg, Louis. *Letters of Louis Wollenberg Written in German During the Decade 1859–1869, Translated into English in Germany in 1939 and Transmitted for Identification To His Son Charles M. Wollenberg.* San Francisco, CA: Grabhorn Press, 1941.

Work Projects Administration. *Journal of the Pioneer and Walker Mining Districts, 1863–1866.* Phoenix, AZ: Archival and Records Project, Historical Records Survey, 1941.

Zeckendorf, William. *Zeckendorf: The Autobiography of William Zeckendorf.* New York: Holt, Rinehart and Winston, 1970.

Secondary Sources—Books

Abrams, Jeanne E. *Jewish Women Pioneering the Frontier Trail: A History in the American West.* New York: New York University Press, 2006.

Alexander, Thomas G. *A Clash of Interests: Interior Department and Mountain West, 1863–1896.* Provo, UT: Brigham Young University Press, 1977.

Arizona Bureau of Mines. *Arizona Lode Gold Mines and Mining.* Bulletin No. 137. Tucson: University of Arizona, 1967.

Bury, John C. *The Historical Role of Arizona's Superintendent of Public Instruction.* 2 vols. Flagstaff: Northern Arizona University, 1974.

Chanin, Abraham. *Cholent and Chorizo.* Tucson, AZ: Midbar Press, 1995.

Cleere, Jan. *Levi's & Lace: Arizona Women Who Made History.* Tucson, AZ: Rio Nuevo Publishers, 2011.

Cleland, Robert Glass. *A History of Phelps Dodge.* New York: Alfred A. Knopf, 1952.

Colquhoun, James. *The Early History of the Clifton-Morenci District.* London: William Clowes and Sons, Ltd., n.d.

———. *The History of the Clifton-Morenci Mining District.* London: John Murray, 1924.

Connelley, William Elsey. *Doniphan's Expedition and the Conquest of New Mexico and California.* Topeka, KS: Published by the author, 1907.

DeArment, Robert K. *Deadly Dozen: Forgotten Gunfighters of the Old West.* 3 vols. Norman: University of Oklahoma Press, 2010.

Dunning, Charles H., and Edward Peplow Jr. *Rock to Riches: The Story of American Mining…Past, Present and Future as Reflected in the Colorful History of Mining in Arizona, the Nation's Greatest Bonanza.* Phoenix, AZ: Southwest Publishing Company, Inc., 1959.

Eppinga, Jane. *Nogales: Life and Times on the Frontier.* Charleston, SC: Arcadia Publishing, 2002.

Farrish, Thomas E. *History of Arizona.* 8 vols. Phoenix, AZ: 1915.

Fierman, Floyd. *Some Early Jewish Settlers on the Southwestern Frontier.* El Paso: Texas Western Press, 1960.

Grasse, David. *The Bisbee Massacre: Robbery, Murder and Retribution in the Arizona Territory, 1883–1884.* Jefferson, NC: McFarland & Company, 2017.

Half a Century, 1884–1934. Holbrook, AZ: Tribune News, 1934.

Ham, Emily Jacobson. *New Frontiers: Jewish Pioneers in the Arizona Territory.* Phoenix: Arizona Jewish Historical Society, 2012.

Harte, John Bret. *Tucson: Portrait of a Desert Pueblo.* Woodland Hills, CA: Windsor Publications, 1980.

Henson, Pauline. *Founding a Wilderness Capital: Prescott, A.T., 1864.* Flagstaff, AZ: Northland Press, 1965.

Hopkins, Ernest J. *Financing the Frontier: A Fifty Year History of the Valley National Bank, 1899–1949.* Phoenix, AZ: Valley National Bank, 1950.

Johnston, Francis J. *The Bradshaw Trail: Narrative and Notes.* Riverside, CA: Historical Commission Press, n.d.

Kelly, George. *Legislative History: Arizona, 1864–1912.* Phoenix, AZ: Manufacturing Stationers, 1926.

Lake, Stuart. *Wyatt Earp: Frontier Marshal.* Boston: Houghton Mifflin, 1931.

Lamar, Howard R. *The Far Southwest, 1846–1912: A Territorial History.* New York: W.W. Norton & Co., 1970.

Learsi, Rufus. *The Jews in America: A History.* New York: KTAV Publishing House, 1972.

Lockwood, Frank C., and Donald W. Page. *Tucson: The Old Pueblo.* Phoenix, AZ: Manufacturing Stationers, 1930.

Love, Frank. *Mining Camps and Ghost Towns: A History of Mining in Arizona and California Along the Lower Colorado.* Los Angeles: Westernlore Press, 1974.

Lyons, Bettina O'Neil. *Zeckendorfs and Steinfelds: Merchant Princes of the American Southwest.* Tucson: Arizona Historical Society, 2008.

Marcus, Jacob R. *The American Jewish Woman, 1654–1980.* New York: KTAV Publishing House, 1981.

McClintock, James H. *Mormon Settlement in Arizona: A Record of Peaceful Conquest of the Desert.* Phoenix, AZ: Manufacturing Stationers, 1921.

Miller, Darliss. *Frontier Army in the Far West.* St. Louis, MO: Forum Press, 1979.

Myrick, David. *Railroads of Arizona*, vol. 2. *Phoenix and the Central Roads.* 3 vols. San Diego, CA: Howell-North Books, 1980.

Parsons, A. B. *The Porphyry Coppers.* New York: American Institute of Mining and Metallurgical Engineers, 1933.

Patton, James. *History of Clifton.* Clifton, AZ: Greenlee Chamber of Commerce, 1977.

Peterson, Charles S. *Take Up Your Mission: Mormon Colonizing Along the Little Colorado River, 1870–1900.* Tucson: University of Arizona Press, 1973.

Ramenofsky, Elizabeth. *From Charcoal to Banking: The I.E. Solomons of Arizona.* Tucson, AZ: Westernlore Press, 1984.

Ready, Alma. *Open Range and Hidden Silver: Arizona's Santa Cruz County.* Nogales, AZ: Alto Press, 1973.

Rickard, T.A. *A History of American Mining.* New York: McGraw Hill Book Company, 1932.

———. *The Romance of Mining.* Toronto: Macmillan Company of Canada, 1945.

Roberts, Gary L. *Doc Holliday: The Life and Legend.* Hoboken, NJ: John Wiley & Sons, Inc., 2006.

Rochlin, Harriet, and Fred Rochlin. *Pioneer Jews: A New Life in the Far West.* Boston: Houghton Mifflin Company, 2000.

Sacks, B. *Arizona's Angry Man: United States Marshal Milton B. Duffield.* Tempe: Arizona Historical Foundation, 1970.

Shillingberg, William B. *Tombstone, A.T.: A History of Early Mining, Milling and Mayhem.* Spokane, WA: Arthur H. Clark Company, 1999.

Sipos, Ed. *Brewing Arizona: A Century of Beer in the Grand Canyon State.* Tucson: University of Arizona Press, 2013.

Smith, Dean. *The Goldwaters of Arizona.* Flagstaff, AZ: Northland Press, 1986.

Sonnichsen, C.L. *Tucson: The Life and Times of an American City.* Norman: University of Oklahoma Press, 1982.

Stanley, Jerry. *Frontier Merchants: Lionel and Barron Jacobs and the Jewish Pioneers Who Settled the West.* New York: Crown Publishers, 1998.

Theobald, John, and Lillian Theobald. *Wells Fargo in Arizona Territory.* Tempe: Arizona Historical Foundation, 1978.

Thrapp, Dan L. *Encyclopedia of Frontier Biography.* 3 vols. Glendale, CA: Arthur H. Clark Company, 1988.

Vorspan, Max, and Lloyd P. Gartner. *History of the Jews of Los Angeles.* San Marino, CA: Huntington Library, 1970.

Wagoner, Jay J. *Arizona Territory, 1863–1912: A Political History.* Tucson: University of Arizona Press, 1970.

Zucker, Robert E. *Treasures of the Santa Catalina Mountains.* Tucson, AZ: BZB Publishing, 2014.

Secondary Sources—Articles

"Abe Goldbaum and the General: An Incident of the Old West." *American Jewish Archives*, April 1957.

Barney, James W. "Rivermen of the Colorado." *Arizona Sheriff*, December 1955.

Carmichael, Norman. "Development of Mine Transportation." *Arizona Mining Journal*, December 1, 1924.

Dworkin, Mark. "Henry Jaffa and Wyatt Earp: Wyatt Earp's Jewish Connection." *New Mexico Historical Society*, December 2005–September 2006.

Fierman, Floyd. "The Drachmans of Arizona." *American Jewish Archives*, November 1964.

———. "The Goldberg Brothers: Arizona Pioneers." *American Jewish Archives*, 1966.

Fulton, Richard W., and Conrad J. Bahre. "Charleston, Arizona: A Documentary Reconstruction." *Arizona and the West*, Spring 1967.

Goldberg, Richard. "Michael Wormser: Capitalist." *American Jewish Archives*, November 1973

Golden, Richard, and Arlene Golden. "The Mark I. Jacobs Family: A Discursive Overview." *Western States Jewish Historical Quarterly*, January 1981.

Greenwood, N.H. "Sol Barth: A Jewish Settler on the Arizona Frontier." *Journal of Arizona History*, Winter 1973.

Haskett, Bert. "History of the Sheep Industry in Arizona." *Arizona Historical Review*, July 1936.

Jeffrey, R. Brooks. "Arizona's First Synagogue: A Story of Birth and Renewal at the Stone Avenue Temple." *Heritage Matters*, December 2003.

Lamont, Marian S. "Jacob Mansfeld—Builder of a Dream." *Chicago Jewish Forum*, Winter 1953–1954.

Landau, Francine. "Solomon Lazard of Los Angeles." *Western States Jewish Historical Quarterly*, April 1973.

Miller, Darliss. "Civilians and Military Supply in the Southwest." *Journal of Arizona History*, Summer 1982.

Monahan, Sherry. "Restaurateur Ike Clanton." *True West*, October 2017.

Rochlin, Harriet. "Brides for Brethren: Arizona Territory, 1854–1883." *Arizona Post*, December 26, 1980.

Rochlin, Harriet, and Fred Rochlin. "Tacking Leopold Ephraim." *Western States Jewish Historical Quarterly*, January 1969.

Rollins, Ralph. "The Life Story of Black Jack Newman." *Mining Journal*, August 30, 1929.

Stanley, Gerald. "Merchandising in the Southwest: The Mark I. Jacobs Company of Tucson, 1867–1875." *American Jewish Archives*, April 1971.

Stern, Norton, and William Kramer. "Arizona's Mining Wizard: Black Jack Newman." *Western States Jewish Historical Quarterly*, April 1979.

Stern, Norton. "Herman Bendell: Superintendent of Indian Affairs, Arizona Territory, 1871–1873." *Western States Jewish Historical Quarterly*, Spring 1976.

———. "Mayor Strauss of Tucson." *Western States Jewish Historical Quarterly*, July 1980.

Toll, William. "The Jewish Merchant and Civic Order in the Urban West." In *Jewish Life in the American West: Perspectives on Migration, Settlement and Community*, edited by Ava Kahn. Los Angeles, CA: Autry Museum of Western Heritage, 2002.

Walker, Henry P. "Wagon Freighting in Arizona." *Smoke Signal* no. 28 (Fall 1973).

Secondary Sources—Theses and Dissertations

Bridenstine, Don C. "Commercial Banking in Arizona—Past and Present." PhD dissertation, University of Southern California, 1958.

Harte, John Bret. "The San Carlos Indian Reservation, 1872–1886: An Administrative History." PhD dissertation, University of Arizona, 1972.

Kushner, Gilbert. "The Jewish Community in Tucson: Structures and Form of Jewish Self-Identification." Master's thesis, University of Arizona, 1958.

Renner, Pamela P. "La Paz—Gateway to Territorial Arizona." Master's thesis, Arizona State University, 1974.

Santiago, Dawn. "The Banking Operations of Lionel and Barron Jacobs in Tucson, 1867–1913." Master's thesis, University of Arizona, 1988.

Spude, Robert L. "Mineral Frontier in Transition: Copper Mining in Arizona, 1880–1885." Master's thesis, Arizona State University, 1976.

Wayte, Harold G. "A History of Holbrook and the Little Colorado Country." Master's thesis, University of Arizona, 1962.

Online Sources

Ascarza, William. "MINE TALES: Quijotoa Boom Years Short Lived." July 26, 2015. tuscon.com.

Deremo, Rhiannon. "Jim Leavy: Gunfighter." *True West*, January 16, 2017. truewestmagazine.com.

Jewish Women's Archives. "Anna F. Solomon." jwa.org.

Mining and Minerals Education Foundation. "Henry Lesinsky." https://miningeducationfoundation.org.

Officer Down Memorial Page. "Deputy Sheriff Kiv Phillips." odmp.org.

Peachin, Mary Levy. "How Levy's Became a Department Store Icon." Inside Tucson Business, June 3, 2011. insidetucsonbusiness.com.

———. "Remembering Douglas's Forgotten Pioneer Jews along the Mexican Border." Arizona Jewish Post, April 3, 2020. azjewishpost.com.

Southwest Jewish Archives. "The Drachman Brothers." https://swja.arizona.edu.

Sullivan, Jack. "Julius Goldbaum: Arizona's Pioneer Whiskey Man." Those Pre-Pro Whiskey Men! March 7, 2017. pre-prowhiskeymen.blogspot.com.

Wright, Erik. "James Leavy: Here Is Our Game." Historynet, February 2015. historynet.com.

ABOUT THE AUTHOR

 A native of San Diego, California, Blaine Lamb received his BA and MA in history from the University of San Diego and his doctorate from Arizona State University. He served as archivist for the California State Railroad Museum and for the California State Archives in Sacramento. He later worked for California State Parks and at the time of his retirement was chief of its Cultural Resources Division. In addition to writing, he enjoys traveling, collecting toy soldiers and working on his model railroad. Blaine's publications include articles and reviews in *California History*, *Western Historical Quarterly*, *Journal of America's Military Past*, *Overland Journal* and *True West*. He is the author of *The Extraordinary Life of Charles Pomeroy Stone: Soldier, Surveyor, Pasha, Engineer*, published in 2016.

Visit us at
www.historypress.com
....